Training Circular
No. TC 7-21

Headquarters
Department of the Army
Washington, DC 1 December 2006

Stryker Driver Training

Contents

DISTRIBUTION RESTRICTION: Approved for public release; distribution is unlimited.

Preface

This training circular (TC) provides standardized driver training and testing for Stryker operators in accordance with AR 600-55, *The Army Driver and Operator Standardization Program*. It teaches novice (inexperienced) and apprentice (one year of military vehicle driving experience) drivers to operate the Stryker vehicle. An apprentice driver may learn to operate the Stryker in less time than the novice, assuming skills learned on other military vehicles are transferable to Stryker operation. Leaders must emphasize driver training because high-technology Stryker vehicles demand greater driver skills and knowledge. This TC does not include any theater-unique requirements. It stresses hands-on training with *minimal* classroom instruction.

Stryker drivers must know how to operate the vehicle's equipment effectively in all environments. They must be challenged to use safe driving practices and increase their awareness of accident avoidance. This TC is designed to accommodate these skills by providing:

- Leadership tools needed to meet the challenge of producing quality Stryker drivers.
- An introduction to Stryker simulated training.
- Guidance on the use and accessing of lesson outlines.
- Written and hands-on performance tests.
- Listings of supporting training materials for all Stryker vehicles.
- The latest techniques to enhance Stryker driver driving skills.
- Slat armor attachment.

TC 7-21 is organized into the following eight chapters and four appendixes that provide Stryker driver training strategies and training support materials:

- Chapter 1, Introduction, explains the purposes, focus, and contents of the manual.
- Chapter 2, Driver Selection, Training, and Supervision, describes a system for identifying, selecting, and qualifying Stryker vehicle drivers.
- Chapter 3, Safety Awareness, examines the safeguards necessary to ensure vehicle operators do not place the physical well-being of people in jeopardy.
- Chapter 4, Environmental Awareness, examines the safeguards necessary to ensure the environment is not placed in jeopardy by vehicle operators.
- Chapter 5, How to Use Training Support Packages (TSPs), describes the learning objectives of TSPs and how to access them for use.
- Chapter 6, Stryker Drivers Vision Enhancer AN/VAS-5, explains Stryker driver use of the DVE.
- Chapter 7, Stryker Driver Trainer, explains Stryker driver use of the Stryker Driver Trainer.
- Chapter 8, Driving with Slat Armor, describes the vehicle's attachable armor commonly in use.
- Appendix A, Stryker Combat Vehicle Driver TSPs, lists all available TSPs.
- Appendix B, Sample Operator/Driver Training Schedule Calendar (10 Day), contains a sample training calendar for adaptation and use.
- Appendix C, Stryker Driver Training Courses, discusses training course design and procedures.
- Appendix D, Lessons Learned, uses a Stryker-comparable U.S. Marine Lessons Learned LAV report of experiences in Iraq.

To effectively execute this TC each instructor should ensure their Stryker operators are trained and tested to the standards contained within it. Graduates (licensed drivers) of this Stryker driver training program should be supervised until they gain the experience necessary to operate safely. Recent graduates should not be placed in situations that exceed their skill levels. Supervisors should periodically ride with each driver to observe safe operating procedures, and to determine any need for additional training.

This publication applies to the Active Army, the Army National Guard/Army National Guard of the United States, and the United States Army Reserve unless otherwise stated.

The proponent of this publication is the United States Army Training and Doctrine Command (TRADOC). The preparing agency is the United States Army Infantry School (USAIS).

RECOMMENDED CHANGES

Users of this training circular are encouraged to recommend changes and make comments for improvement. Any comments should note the specific page, paragraph, and line where a change is recommended. Please add reasons for each comment so your recommended change will be understood and completely evaluated. Detailed revision suggestions should be submitted on DA Form 2028 (Recommended Changes to Publications and Blank Forms) to:

Email: systems.div@benning.army.mil

Phone: COM 706-545-1619 or DSN 835-1619

Phone: COM 706-545-1619 or DSN 835-16190

Commandant
U.S. Army Infantry School
6751 Constitutioin Loop, Bldg 4
ATTN: ATSH-DOT
Fort Benning, Georgia 31905-5593

Unless otherwise stated, whenever the masculine gender is used, both men and women are implied.

Chapter 1

Introduction

Stryker drivers must know how to operate vehicle equipment effectively in all environments. They must be challenged to use safe driving practices and increase their awareness for accident avoidance. This chapter addresses these important driver needs and materials available to accommodate training.

PURPOSE

1-1. Developed as a supplement to AR 600-55, *The Army Driver and Operator Standardization Program*, TC 7-21 provides performance tests and lists of supporting training materials for all Stryker vehicles. Its purpose is to assist leaders in meeting the challenge of producing quality Stryker vehicle drivers.

SCOPE

1-2. Leaders must emphasize driver training because high-technology, high-performance Stryker vehicles demand excellent driver skills. TC 7-21 does not replace AR 600-55, which specifies the regulatory requirements for selecting, training, testing, and licensing drivers. This training circular provides guidance on specific Stryker vehicle training with emphasis on operation and safety. The need for initial and concurrent Stryker driver training has produced several Stryker driver training support packages (TSPs); so this TC discusses their teaching format and TSP access. Unit constraints on terrain and resources may limit the extent to which a TSP can be implemented. To accommodate this, unit commanders have the flexibility to make minor TSP modifications. Regardless of any modifications, drivers must pass the required TSP tests to be issued an OF 346 standard or limited permit (IAW AR 600-55, chapter 6).

SUPPORTING MATERIALS

1-3. The supporting materials unique to each Stryker vehicle are listed at the end of the training support packages. The following materials apply to all Stryker vehicles.

   (1) AR 600-55, *The Army Driver and Operator Standardization Program* (*Selection, Training, Testing, and Licensing*), 31 December 1993. This regulation describes the following:

   - Responsibilities for conducting the motor vehicle driver program.
   - Licensing requirements for applicants of motor vehicle driver positions.
   - The process for choosing potential drivers.
   - The training program for drivers of all types of vehicles and equipment.
   - The testing program.
   - Controls on issuing licenses.
   - Types of licenses that may be issued.
   - Procedures for renewing, revoking, or suspending licenses.
   - Procedures for qualifying operators to use special equipment and night vision devices.

   (2) Soldier Training Publications. The individual tasks in this TC's training support packages were derived from Soldier training publications developed for Stryker vehicles.

   (3) AR 385-55, *Prevention of Motor Vehicle Accidents*, 12 March 1987. This regulation establishes responsibilities and procedures for carrying out the Army Safety Program's motor vehicle accident prevention effort.

(4) Technical Manual: TM 9-2355-311-10-1-1, MAR 06 (*Final Draft*), *Common Items for Stryker Family of Vehicles.*

CONTENTS

1-4.   Contents in this training circular are designed to provide training information, strategies, program development, and training support materials for Stryker driver training. Leaders will receive relevant information to assist the development of individual training programs. Everything from instructor/driver selection—to driver tactics, techniques, and procedures are covered in the pages that follow. Working together with available TSPs, TC 7-21 can improve your unit driver skills.

1-5.   The information contained in this publication is applicable to all active Army, Army Reserve, and National Guard units that use Stryker vehicles.

Figure 1-1. Infantry carrier vehicle

Chapter 2

Driver Selection, Training, and Supervision

This chapter outlines a system (described in detail in AR 600-55) for identifying, selecting, and qualifying trainers and drivers. The Army vehicle driver's contribution to combat efficiency is not always recognized or appreciated. Nevertheless, driver performance is critical to keeping a vehicle in the fight. Poor driver training can cause a unit to fail in its mission. Even the best-designed vehicles maintained by the best Army operators and mechanics cannot compensate for poor driving practices. Therefore, quality trainer and driver selection is crucial to Army goals.

PREPARATION FOR DRIVER TRAINING

2-1.   Effective driver training is the result of careful planning and thorough instruction. Before instruction begins, a careful and complete estimate of driver training requirements must be made. Next, plans and schedules must be developed; selected instructors must be trained; and adequate facilities and equipment must be located. Students should be made aware of all relevant regulations during the first phase of training. To accommodate this, units should have a current file of all Army, post, and unit publications and policies that pertain to driver training.

ESTIMATE OF DRIVER TRAINING SITUATION

2-2.   When preparing to conduct a driver training program, an estimate of the driver training situation should be made by answering the following:
- (1)   How many personnel require qualification (monthly/annually)?
- (2)   How many previously licensed drivers need verification or recertification?
- (3)   What are the capabilities and general experiences of new drivers who need qualification?
- (4)   What are the seasonal requirements for unit location?
- (5)   How much time is available?
- (6)   What type of wheeled-vehicle accidents has the unit experienced?
- (7)   How many instructors are available?
- (8)   Will the training be part of unit in-processing?
- (9)   What special training do the instructors require?
- (10)   What facilities, supplies, and equipment (including training aids, vehicles, and driving ranges with varied terrain) are available?
- (11)   What major training events are scheduled for the unit?

2-3.   Answers to these questions should then be analyzed to help develop and organize an effective training plan. The appropriate TSPs should be analyzed to determine the following:
- (1)   The number of instructors who need training and a schedule for their instruction.
- (2)   The duties and responsibilities of each instructor.
- (3)   The number of drivers who require training or retraining and a schedule for their instruction.
- (4)   How students will be grouped and how each group will be rotated.
- (5)   What facilities, supplies, and equipment are needed and how to get them ready.
- (6)   The standards for training required by the appropriate TSP and your unit's needs.

INSTRUCTOR SELECTION

2-4.   Battalion-level officers are normally responsible for the selection and training of instructors. Selection of the best NCOs for positions as vehicle drivers, maintenance personnel, and instructors is crucial. All prospective instructors should—

- Be competent and well trained in their military occupation skills.
- Be qualified to operate the equipment
- Have been licensed on the equipment for at least one year.
- Have technical knowledge of the equipment.
- Have the knowledge and experience necessary to instruct.

INSTRUCTOR TRAINING

2-5. Instructors should be given refresher training to sharpen their skills and help them become more proficient instructors. It may not be necessary for instructors to take the entire course students receive. However, the entire course must be covered to make sure instructors are familiar with all teaching points. Refresher training should cover—
  (1) Army, state, local, installation, and unit driving regulations.
  (2) Safe driving procedures.
  (3) Seasonal hazards.
  (4) Operator maintenance and use of the training vehicle's operator manual.

2-6. Emphasis should be placed on the importance of observing student driving techniques so errors can be corrected immediately.

2-7. Instructors must be specially trained to administer the physical qualifications, written, and performance tests. Prior to administration instructors must understand the purpose and nature of each test. They should thoroughly understand each examination's standards and scoring requirements. (This information will be outlined in the TAG for each examination.) They must also adhere to the test administration guide(s) (TAG) in the TSPs.

DRIVER SELECTION

SELECT THE BEST-QUALIFIED PERSONNEL (AR 600-55)

2-8. Poor drivers often cause a loss of valuable unit training time through produced injuries (to themselves and others), or equipment damage. Therefore, poor training risks should be identified and eliminated before training starts. When selecting personnel for training as Stryker vehicle drivers, it is best to pick those with previous driving experience. When this is not possible, Soldiers with no previous driving experience can be selected, if the requirements are met. Once a driver is selected, information obtained from the interview, battery tests, physical qualification tests, and the road test should be recorded on DA Form 348. (For proper use of this form, see AR 600-55.)

RECORDS REVIEW

2-9. The commander or his designated representative will review the following records:
  (1) DA Form 348 (Equipment Operator's Qualification Record [Except Aircraft]).
  (2) Medical profiles.

INTERVIEW

2-10. After reviewing the records, an interview will reveal useful information about the individual under consideration. During the interview, any characteristics that might affect driver performance should be noted.

2-11. Areas of concern include:
- Maturity.
- Attitude.
- Past driving record.
- Hearing.
- Extreme nervousness.

- Any abnormal characteristics.
- Medication (used regularly) that causes drowsiness, impairs vision, or affects coordination. (Check with medical personnel regarding concerns about medication.)

2-12. Suggested questions for the interview should include:

- How much experience have you had in driving a passenger car?
- How many miles have you driven during the past 12 months?
- Have you ever driven a combat vehicle?
- Have you operated any heavy equipment such as tractors, road graders, or bulldozers? If so, for how long?
- How much experience have you had driving a truck of 1/2-ton or greater capacity?
- Have you ever driven a truck with all-wheel drive?
- Have you had an accident in which someone was injured or property damage exceeded $1,000? If so, explain who was at fault, and how, in your opinion, the accident could have been avoided.
- Have you had any traffic violations?
- How do you account for your good or bad driving record?
- Do you think you would make a good Stryker vehicle driver? Why?
- Can you repair automobiles or related machinery? If so, what is your experience with this sort of work?
- Do you have any problems with your eyes that would affect your driving ability (day or night)? Do you wear corrective lenses?
- Do you have any hearing problems?
- Do you know of any physical problems that might affect your ability to drive?
- Have you ever been involved in a drug or alcohol offense?

PHYSICAL EVALUATION MEASURES

GENERAL

2-13. All military personnel are required to undergo periodic medical examinations according to AR 40-501, *Standards of Medical Fitness*. AR 600-55 requires all potential military drivers to undergo physical qualification tests. The purpose of these tests is to ensure operators of military motor vehicles possess at least minimum physical requirements for safe driving. They are also intended for diagnostic, guidance, and counseling purposes. AR 600-55 describes the procedures for administering the physical qualification tests in detail. The test's primary components follow.

EQUIPMENT

2-14. The portable driver testing and training device contains all materials necessary to conduct a physical qualifications test. This equipment can be requisitioned through supply channels. If assistance is required, the post safety officer can properly identify the vehicle model and training source of supply. Equivalent testing instruments may be constructed locally, provided they are made to accurately measure the physical characteristics prescribed in the following paragraphs.

TESTING CONDITIONS

2-15. The general conditions of the test situation are prescribed in Section III, AR 611-5. Rooms in which the tests are given must be well lighted (without glare), and well ventilated. The examinee should be made comfortable so physical discomfort does not affect test results. If it is necessary to test multiple examinees simultaneously in the same room, distractions during testing should be kept to a minimum. The reaction time test must be given under conditions that are free from noise and other distractions.

SUPPLEMENTARY INSTRUCTIONS TO EXAMINERS

2-16. The following instructions apply to all physical evaluation testing and supplement the specific instructions accompanying the equipment.

(1) Before giving any test, become knowledgeable on the purpose of the test, the equipment to be used, and the prescribed procedure. Give a number of trial tests to become familiar with the test and test procedures.

(2) Before each test, explain its purpose and what examinees should expect.

(3) Measure physical characteristics in the order they are listed in the following paragraphs.

(4) Record measurements on DA Form 348, Equipment Operator's Qualification Record (Except Aircraft), or an equivalent official form.

(5) On completion of testing, inform examinees of any discovered physical limitations.

(6) Describe compensating measures that may be taken.

PHYSICAL CHARACTERISTICS TO BE TESTED

2-17. The following instructions apply to all physical evaluation testing.

VISUAL ACUITY

- *Purpose.* Determine whether the examinee can see well enough to drive safely.

- *Minimum standard.* Uncorrected distant visual acuity of any degree that is correctable to not less than 20/40 with a numerical designator of "l," "2," or "3" under the "E" factor of the physical profile serial. Tested with both eyes open, a visual acuity of 20/40 must be attainable with corrective lenses. All Army drivers who require corrective lenses to attain 20/40 visual acuity are required to wear corrective lenses while operating Army vehicles. Operator permits must be annotated to reflect this requirement.

FIELD OF VISION

- *Purpose.* Determine whether the examinee can see to the side while looking straight ahead.

- *Minimum standard.* A lateral range of 75 percent on each side of the focus line is the minimum standard acceptable for each eye. If the standard is not met, the examinee will be referred to appropriate medical personnel to determine if his lateral vision is sufficient for safe driving.

DEPTH PERCEPTION

- *Purpose.* Determine how well the examinee can judge distances.

- *Minimum standard.* None; the results of this measure are used in driver counseling and training.

COLOR PERCEPTION

- *Purpose.* Determine if the examinee is color-blind.

- *Minimum standard.* The examinee will not be disqualified for a vehicle operator's license because of color-blindness. However, examinees who test color-blind will be given additional training on traffic light sequence and traffic observation to assist safe driving.

FOOT REACTION TIME

- *Purpose.* Determine whether the examinee can move his foot quickly enough in response to driving conditions.

- *Minimum standard.* Reaction time up to and including 0.60 second is acceptable. If the examinee's reaction time is faster than 0.40 second, he will be cautioned about the possibility of rear-end collisions with following drivers whose reaction times are much slower. Any sudden application of brakes could invite such a collision with a slower reacting driver. If the examinee's reaction time is between 0.50 and 0.60 seconds, he will be made aware of this slower time and advised to allow extra following distance to compensate for the deficiency. If the reaction time of the examinee is slower than 0.60 second, he will be referred to medical personnel for a professional driving status decision.

HEARING TEST

- *Purpose.* Determine whether the examinee can hear well enough to drive safely.
- *Minimum standard.* Examinees must attain a numerical designator of "1" or "2" under the "H" factor of the physical profile serial to unconditionally pass the hearing test. Those scoring a "3" or "4" will be referred to medical personnel for a professional driving status decision. All driver personnel are required to have an annual hearing conservation examination.

TRAINING PROGRAM

2-18. The commander develops his training strategy after assessing the strengths and weaknesses of his unit. The assessment must include any personnel turbulence (changes). His strategy must focus on his METL, sustain his unit's strengths, and correct its weaknesses. He will find that some tasks apply to Soldiers generally, and that others apply exclusively to Soldiers in a squad. These factors require an integrated training strategy. Vehicle commanders are proficient with all tasks performed on the vehicle, just as drivers are proficient with all driver tasks. However, squad members who are trained to be proficient on all vehicle tasks, including driving, will function better as a team.

BASIC DRIVER TRAINING

2-19. Basic driver training develops individual skills needed to operate the vehicle. The driver is trained and evaluated on—

- Performing all preventive maintenance checks and services on the hull.
- Performing offensive and defensive driving techniques.
- Performing recovery operations.
- Performing day and night driving techniques.
- Performing crew and squad drills.

STRYKER DRIVER TRAINER

2-20. The Stryker Driver Trainer (CDT/SV) allows simulated training in multiple environments without the expense of using the actual vehicle. Training focuses on driver coordination and tasks such as ground guide railhead operations, and unusual driving conditions.

ADVANCED DRIVER TRAINING

2-21. Advanced driver training develops specific skills needed to operate the vehicle in extreme or unusual conditions.

Drivers are trained and evaluated on—

- Operating the vehicle in combat conditions.
- Operating the vehicle in unusual terrain or environmental conditions.
- Operating the vehicle with slat armor or with combat weight.
- Performing high speed driving techniques.
- Performing evasive driving techniques.

CROSS-TRAINING

2-22. Cross-training enhances the coordination between the vehicle crew and squad. It must occur as often as possible because it is critical to countering personnel losses in peacetime or combat. Effective cross-training incorporates the individual and squad to sustain basic crew skills. It also provides additional training so squad members can perform as Stryker drivers.

TRAINING PLANS

2-23. Once the commander has developed his METL and thoroughly assessed training proficiency, he begins the detailed process of developing a training plan.

MASTER DRIVER

2-24. The primary mission of the Master Driver is to train vehicle drivers. The Master Driver helps commanders at all echelons plan, develop, execute, and evaluate all driver-related training.

2-25. Directed by the commander in his specific responsibilities, the Master Driver—

(1) Assists the validation or certification of newly assigned Soldiers.

(2) Sets up or conducts initial skills training for new drivers.

(3) Trains and certifies driver training evaluators.

(4) Assists all elements in the unit concerning drivers training.

(5) Forecasts all resources for training.

(6) Manages driver records.

(7) Coordinates and controls training device use.

(8) If SIO (senior instructor/operator) qualified, he certifies and recertifies other I/Os to conduct Stryker Driver Trainer training.

(9) Plans and manages simulation training.

(10) Executes driver training.

(11) Assists in training new drivers.

CREW STABILITY MANAGEMENT

2-26. The greatest problem a commander must contend with in developing a training plan is personnel turbulence (personnel changes). He must develop a plan to reduce and control it before developing and executing his training plan. This turbulence is inevitable. However, he can reduce it with short- or long-term solutions.

Short-term Solutions

(1) Change personnel as a crew rather than a single crewman.

(2) Train an alternate for each position.

Long-Term Solutions

(1) Continually cross-train personnel for replacements. Experienced Soldiers are easier to train than new Soldiers.

(2) Form complete crews as personnel come into the unit. Match the loss dates (ETS, PCS, and DEROS) within the same crew.

TRAINING CONDITIONS

2-27. Driving and operational conditions vary so crews learn to fight in any battlefield environment. Training in a variety of conditions ensures crews can perform in adverse weather and degraded mode operations. Thermal sights must be used not only at night, but also during daylight operations in smoke, adverse weather conditions, and concealing terrain.

ADVERSE WEATHER

2-28. Soldiers must know how adverse weather affects their senses. They must also know how to mechanically operate the weapons system.

(1) Fog, snow, and heavy rain hinder target acquisition, range determination, and burst on target (BOT).

(2) Temperature extremes and humidity affect cyclic rates of fire and ballistics.

DEGRADED MODE TRAINING

2-29. Squads must be trained to function with less than a fully operational system in less than normal operating conditions.

(1) Battle damage and maintenance problems can deny the use of primary vehicle control systems. Squads must continue the fight using degraded mode operations.

(2) NBC conditions severely influence the squad's ability to—

- Operate the controls and perform individual duties.
- Observe through the optics and sensors.
- Perform during continuous operations.

DRIVER INCENTIVE PROGRAMS

2-30. Army policy encourages incentive awards programs to motivate personnel in skills improvement. Every organization should have an incentive awards program for its drivers to ensure they receive recognition for their efforts. Competitive operator maintenance inspections, obstacle driving, and vehicle maneuvers are a few programs the commander may initiate. These events give drivers a chance to demonstrate their abilities. They also give the commander a chance to evaluate the unit's overall driver training program. Expert driver badges or certificates presented to qualified drivers give them due recognition. To emphasize the importance of these awards, the commander should present them during a ceremony or formation. Award requirements can be found in AR 600-8-22.

PROGRAM ADMINISTRATION

2-31. Publications, forms, historical records, and reports are part of daily operations. Forms and publications used at the unit level should be part of the driver training program to ensure proper management control and compliance with maintenance procedures. These forms are covered in detail in AR 600-8-22. Both the commander and trainer must be familiar with the publications that govern driving Army vehicles. The manuals listed in the references section are necessary to properly manage and supervise the driver training program.

This page intentionally left blank.

Chapter 3

Safety Awareness

Safety instruction is defined in the AR 385-series as a command responsibility. A training program emphasizing safety can prevent loss of life, damage to property and equipment, and personal injury. Safety practices and application must be monitored at all times during the training phase through performance to standards. Much of this information may already be incorporated in unit TSPs for Stryker vehicles. This chapter discusses safety, common causes of vehicle accidents, and the actions drivers, crews, and leaders should take to prevent accidents. Leaders should read this chapter, review TSPs, and where appropriate, supplement safety and environmental instruction for unit drivers.

FORCE PROTECTION

3-1. Safety is a component of force protection. Commanders, leaders, and Soldiers use risk assessment and management to tie force protection into the mission. Risk management assigns responsibility, institutionalizes the commander's review of operational safety, and leads to decisionmaking appropriate to the risk. The objective of safety is to help units protect combat power through accident prevention, which enables units to fight rapidly and decisively with minimum losses. Safety is an integral part of all combat operations. Safety begins with readiness, which determines a unit's ability to perform its mission essential task list (METL) to standard.

3-2. Risk management is a tool that addresses the root causes of accidents (readiness shortcomings). It assists commanders and leaders identify the source of the next accident and who will have it. Risk management is a way to put more realism into training without paying the price in deaths, injuries, or damaged equipment.

3-3. Safety demands total chain of command involvement in planning, preparing, executing, and evaluating training. Chain of command responsibilities follow.

COMMANDERS –
- Seek optimum, not adequate, performance.
- Specify the risk they will accept to accomplish the mission.
- Select risk reductions provided by the staff.
- Accept or reject residual risk, based on the benefit to be derived.
- Train and motivate leaders at all levels to effectively use risk management concepts.

STAFF –
- Assist the commander in assessing risks, and develop risk reduction options for training.
- Integrate risk controls in plans, orders, METL standards, and performance measures.
- Eliminate unnecessary safety restrictions that diminish training effectiveness.
- Assess safety performance during training.
- Evaluate safety performance during after-action reviews (AAR).

SUBORDINATE LEADERS –
- Apply effective risk management concepts and methods consistently to operations they lead.
- Enforce risk management in accordance with the commander's guidance and intent.

   ● Report risk issues beyond their control or authority to their superiors.

INDIVIDUAL SOLDIERS –

   ● Report unsafe conditions and act to correct the situation when possible.
   ● Establish a buddy system to keep a safety watch on one another.
   ● Take responsibility for personal safety.
   ● Work as team members.
   ● Modify individual risk behavior.

3-4.   Risk management is a five-step cyclic process that is easily integrated into the decisionmaking process outlined in FM 100-14. The five steps are:

   (1) *Identify Hazards.* Identify hazards to the force. Consider all aspects of current and future situations, the environment, and known historical problems.

   (2) *Assess Hazards.* Assess hazards using the risk assessment matrix in Figure 1-1. Assess the conditions listed in each category to derive a numeric value where two conditions intersect. Then add the numeric value of each category to determine the *risk value.* This number will represent the level of risk for the operation assessed.

   (3) *Develop Controls and Make Risk Decisions.* Develop controls that eliminate a hazard or reduce its risk. As control measures are developed, risks are reevaluated until all risks are reduced to a level where benefits outweigh potential costs. Accept no unnecessary risks and make any residual risk decisions at the proper level of command.

   (4) *Implement Controls.* Put controls in place to eliminate the hazards or reduce their risk.

   (5) *Supervise and Evaluate.* Enforce standards and controls. Evaluate the effectiveness of controls and adjust/update them as necessary.

NOTE: The Risk Management Training Support Package for Soldiers, developed by the U.S. Army Safety Center, should be used to train personnel on the five-step risk management process and the risk assessment matrix. To obtain this training support package, contact the U.S. Army Safety Center, ATTN: CSSC-RA, Fort Rucker, AL 36362-5363. (E-mail address: http://"CSSC"@safety.army mil)

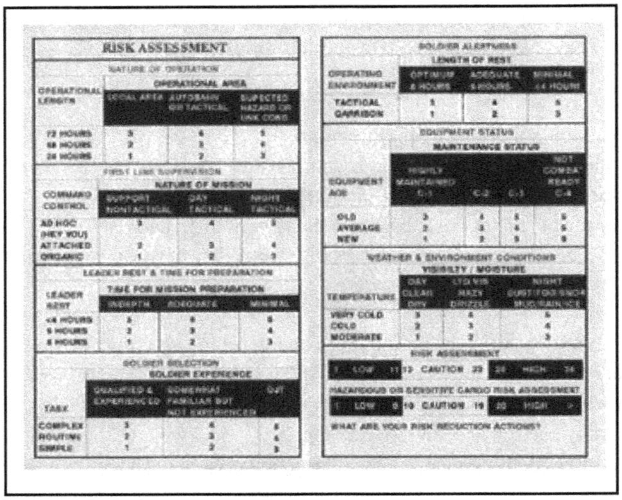

Figure 3-1. Standard risk assessment matrix.

DRIVER RESPONSIBILITIES AND GOVERNMENT LIABILITY

3-5. Soldiers are responsible for operating both tactical and nontactical vehicles in a safe and prudent manner. Failure to operate a vehicle safely in accordance with all driving laws, regulations and procedures can lead to administrative and military justice consequences. Consequences can include reprimand, report of survey, Article 15, or more serious actions. A Soldier can be held financially liable for the damage caused to his vehicle or another Government vehicle. The Government is also responsible for the actions of military vehicle operators. Accidents and property damage caused by Army drivers result in millions of dollars in liability for the Government each year. More dollars for accidents mean fewer dollars for training.

GENERAL SAFETY GUIDELINES

3-6. Everyone in the chain of command should strictly supervise driver training for Stryker vehicle drivers. The following guidelines have proven to be effective when integrated into training and should be included in programs of instruction:

- Conduct a complete and thorough safety briefing before the start of all training sessions.
- Make sure all drivers are trained and licensed to operate their assigned Stryker vehicles. During training, student drivers should have an OF 346 (*U.S. Government Motor Vehicle Operator's Identification Card*) stamped "LEARNER". A licensed instructor must accompany a student driver with a learner's permit when he drives. The student must never be permitted to operate a Stryker vehicle without proper supervision.
- Use caution when driving through towns and villages. Streets are sometimes narrow and difficult to negotiate. If the driver is in doubt, he should stop so the vehicle commander can dismount a ground guide. Pay attention to pedestrians, and be aware that Stryker vehicles draw curious people who have no idea how dangerous the vehicles can be.
- Be aware of vehicle height when entering tunnels, underpasses, and building overhangs close to roadways.
- Beware of icy spots on roadways, especially overpasses, which ice over very quickly.
- Be alert to the presence of overhead power lines. Before driving on roadways, tie down antennas to make sure they do not come in contact with overhead power lines.
- Be aware of steep or excessively rough terrain.
- Make sure drivers understand all road and traffic signals. Despite their size, Stryker vehicles do not always have the right-of-way on roadways.
- Before crossing any bridge or overpass, note the bridge load classification and the height/width limitations of the underpass. If the vehicle exceeds the classification, it cannot cross.

HEARING PROTECTION

3-7. Hearing loss is a concern among Stryker crewmen because of improper fit, wear, and maintenance of combat vehicle crewman (CVC) helmets. Commanders must therefore make sure that each Soldier is properly fitted with a helmet, and that helmets are properly maintained. All crew members will wear CVC helmets. Passengers will wear ear plugs and Kevlar helmets when the vehicle is operating. When the CVC helmet is worn, make sure the chinstrap is fastened. The CVC helmet will not properly reduce sound unless it is fastened. Personnel should also wear hearing protection while performing maintenance on a Stryker vehicle.

COMMUNICATIONS

3-8. Do not move a Stryker vehicle until intercommunications have been established between all crew members. If communications are lost, the vehicle must halt immediately. The crew should troubleshoot the system and notify organizational maintenance if assistance is required. For safety, the unit commander can authorize the movement or removal of the disabled vehicle.

ESCORT VEHICLES

3-9.   A wheeled vehicle with rotating amber warning light(s) (RAWL) should precede a Stryker vehicle or column of Stryker vehicles traveling on a road. On high-speed roads when traffic is normal and enemy contact is not imminent, convoy escort vehicles equipped with RAWLs and required convoy signs or flags should be positioned in the front and rear (IAW with local command policy).

SHOP AND MOTOR POOL

3-10. Certain precautions must be taken in a maintenance shop or motor pool. Oil, water, and antifreeze spills can cause serious injury. To prevent injuries, all spills must be cleaned up immediately, and the work area should be kept clean at all times. Many injuries result from using the wrong tools and equipment. All personnel should therefore be instructed in the proper use of Stryker equipment and tools. All military vehicles must be equipped with chock blocks for use when maintenance is performed and when vehicles are parked on inclines. To prevent severe injuries to fingers, wrists, and limbs, all jewelry must be removed before mounting, dismounting, or performing Stryker maintenance.

HATCH COVERS

3-11. Injuries caused by unsecured hatch covers are common. All crew members must therefore check all hatches before operating a Stryker vehicle to make sure they are serviceable and locked in the proper position. Many vehicles are equipped with chains to secure the hatches. When vehicles are equipped with chains, they must be used.

RIDING POSITION

3-12. Crew members in a Stryker vehicle must wear CVC helmets and ride with only their heads and shoulders extended (name tag defilade) out of the hatches. When a Stryker vehicle collides or overturns, injuries are usually the result of crew members being thrown from the vehicle. If seat belts are installed, they must be worn.

SPEED CONTROL

3-13. Elements in a column of any length may simultaneously encounter many different types of routes and obstacles. This causes different parts of the column to move at varying speeds at the same time. To increase safety and reduce column whipping, the movement or march order should give march speed, vehicle interval, and maximum catch-up speed.

EMERGENCY STOPPING PROCEDURES

3-14. The Stryker driver may have to apply emergency stopping procedures in response to the loss of brakes, steering, or engine power. TMs are available that address emergency stopping procedures. If brake failure occurs, the following seven steps should be performed by a Stryker driver.

WARNING

All crew members must remain inside the vehicle.

---

(1)   Driver notifies the vehicle commander that the brakes have malfunctioned.

(2)   Driver moves the gear select to N (neutral).

(3)   Driver centers the steering column.

(4)   Driver lets the vehicle coast to a stop.

(5)   Driver sets the parking brake if the vehicle has one.

(6)   Driver shuts down the engine once the vehicle has stopped.

(7)   Vehicle commander notifies the chain of command.

MOUNTING AND DISMOUNTING STRYKER VEHICLES

3-15. Commanders and crew members, especially drivers, must make sure the following rules for mounting and dismounting Stryker vehicles are strictly observed by everyone:

- Use extreme caution when mounting or dismounting a vehicle.
- Never climb in front of a weapon to mount the vehicle. Stryker vehicle commanders must make sure that all weapon systems are clear and positioned to allow safe access.
- When mounting or dismounting a vehicle with the engine running, make sure the driver knows personnel are going to mount or dismount. On moving firing ranges, personnel should mount vehicles over the right front fender. Make sure the driver is aware of a crew member's intention to mount.
- Mount the Stryker vehicles from the front (drivers only). Crew members should mount from only the rear.
- Always maintain three points of contact (one hand and two feet or two hands and one foot) with the vehicle when mounting, dismounting, or moving around on the vehicle.
- Never mount or dismount a moving vehicle. Drivers must bring the vehicle to a complete halt before allowing anyone to mount or dismount.
- Never dismount a vehicle by jumping from it.

CREW EVACUATION DRILLS

3-16. Crew evacuation drills are often overlooked during training. The probability of an injury can be significantly reduced if crews practice proper evacuation techniques. Vehicle TMs provide emergency procedures, which should be incorporated into driver and crew training programs.

SLAVE STARTING

3-17. When slave starting a vehicle, always position the live vehicle alongside the dead vehicle. Never position vehicles nose-to-nose. Do not stand between the moving vehicle and the dead vehicle. Serious injury or death could result.

STRYKER VEHICLE ACCIDENTS

FATIGUE AND SLEEP LOSS

3-18. Fatigue and sleep loss are often factors in vehicle accidents. To minimize the effects of sleep loss, commanders must develop and follow a sleep plan based on the following considerations:

- At least five hours sleep is required to enable an individual to maintain optimal performance; humans do not adapt well to shortened sleep cycles.
- Physical strength remains unimpaired until extreme levels of sleep deprivation are reached.
- The most difficult jobs for the sleep-deprived are tasks requiring swift decisions or complex planning.
- Sleep loss typically causes errors of omission.
- Prolonged heat exposure, confinement, noise, and vibration (all of which are present in Stryker vehicles) degrade performance and ability to cope with sleep loss.
- Diminished awareness. Drivers should be checked for symptoms of fatigue or use of controlled substances. Personnel taking prescription drugs that may cause drowsiness should not drive.

Situational Awareness

3-19. To avoid situations conducive to accidental injury and to minimize the possibility of injury in those situations that cannot be avoided, drivers and crew members must be alert at all times. Take extra precautions when the vehicle's metal decks are wet, muddy, or snow covered. They become extremely slippery under those conditions. Likewise, drivers and crew members should remain alert to the position of weapons, hatches, and other metal projections. Accidental contact with these or any other projected objects can result in serious injury.

Blind Spots

3-20. Stryker vehicles have blind spots where the hull blocks the forward or peripheral vision of the driver, preventing him from seeing objects on the ground. The vehicle commander and other crew members should help the driver identify objects in his blind spot. The driver should anticipate approaching objects that may fall into this blind spot as he nears them. If in doubt, the vehicle commander should use a ground guide to assist the driver.

Loss of Control

3-21. Driving too fast for road conditions is the main cause for loss of control in Stryker vehicles. If the driver loses control of his vehicle, he must take immediate steps to regain control. He must release the accelerator, avoid applying the brakes, and let the vehicle coast to a stop. If the vehicle is sliding, the driver must steer in the direction of the skid to regain vehicle control. If the vehicle appears to be sliding or rolling over into a body of water, the driver should attempt to steer into the water to prevent a submerging rollover. The crew is more likely to survive in an upright vehicle than one overturned.

Rollovers

3-22. The safest place for the crew during a rollover is inside the vehicle. If a Stryker vehicle is about to roll over, the driver must alert the crew members so they can drop inside the vehicle and assume a safe position by bracing themselves. The driver must lower his seat and brace himself. Crews must practice rollover procedures.

ACCIDENT PREVENTION

3-23. To prevent accidents, drivers must—
  (1) Adjust speed and interval to allow for wet road surfaces.
  (2) Notify vehicle commander when he is getting sleepy.
  (3) Employ proper techniques to prevent or recover from a skid.
  (4) Be rotated frequently.
  (5) Slow down after dropping off the edge of the roadway before pulling back on the pavement.
  (6) Make sure vehicles have been safety inspected and maintained.
  (7) Use the recommended pumping action in emergencies instead of locking the brakes.
  (8) Allow for the added force of the weight of the vehicle when quick stops are necessary.
  (9) Come to a complete stop and downshift at the crest of steep grades to control speed.
  (10) Know the distance required for braking at various speeds to make emergency stops safely. This factor is especially important for vehicles towing or moving heavy loads.
  (11) React and brake when the brake lights of the vehicle ahead go on. Its driver has already reacted to something and the follow-on vehicles must slow down or stop in the remaining distance.
  (12) After rest stops, inspect beneath vehicles for sleeping personnel.
  (13) Use tow bars rather than cables to move disabled vehicles on roads. If tow cables are used, use a third vehicle of equal weight or heavier as a braking vehicle.
  (14) Inspect personnel heaters to avoid carbon monoxide poisoning.

FIRE PREVENTION

3-24. All crew members must be aware of the danger of fire when operating Stryker vehicles. Flammables and miscellaneous items should not be stored in the vehicle. Leaders should establish some simple rules or an SOP to help prevent fires on vehicles. (For details that apply to a specific vehicle, see the vehicle TM.) However, all crew members must be aware of the danger of fire when operating Stryker vehicles.

3-25. Clean up all gasoline and diesel fuel spills immediately. Use only authorized cleaning agents. Never use gasoline or diesel fuel to clean up spills.

3-26. All Stryker vehicles are equipped with fire extinguishers, both fixed and portable. Crew members must know how and when to use them. To make sure fire extinguishers are ready for instant use, periodically weigh or check them to determine operability. Replace them if necessary.

  (1) *Fixed Fire Extinguishers.* Fixed fire extinguishers that require only the action of a trip handle or sensor to operate are installed on vehicles to cover areas where fires are most likely to start. They should be inspected during the preventive maintenance checks and services, in accordance with the vehicle's TM. Do not start the engine of a Stryker vehicle if the fixed fire extinguishers are inoperable, or if they have been removed for maintenance.

  (2) *Portable Fire Extinguishers.* Portable fire extinguishers are used to fight fires outside the effective range of fixed extinguishers. Portable extinguishers must be manned whenever the vehicle is being refueled. They should be inspected during the preventive maintenance checks and services. If they are inoperable, they should be replaced or refilled before the vehicle is started.

GROUND GUIDES

3-27. Ground guides are needed for safe movement of Stryker vehicles.

WARNING

Using ground guides is so routine that safety rules are sometimes overlooked. This must not happen.

3-28. Train ground guides and drivers in standard arm-and-hand and flashlight signals before guiding or driving Stryker vehicles. Drivers and ground guides must know and observe the following rules:

  (1) Ground guides are required when a Stryker vehicle is moved in a confined or congested area. They are also necessary during limited visibility and when the driver is in doubt about adequate clearance in areas such as narrow bridges and passages with low overhead clearances.

  (2) Ground guides should never stand in front of a vehicle when the engine is running. They should stand beside the right or left fender when talking to and directing the driver.

  (3) Ground guides must be used in cantonments, bivouac sites, and parking areas.

  (4) Ground guides must never run in front of vehicles or walk backwards while guiding vehicles.

  (5) Flashlights with a colored filter should be used when vehicles are moved at night.

  (6) Ground guides should walk 30 feet in front of—and to the left of the left fender—to observe traffic to the front and rear of the vehicles. A ground guide is the correct distance from a Stryker vehicle when the driver can see the ground guide's feet.

  (7) Any time a Stryker vehicle is being moved in reverse and a ground guide is necessary, two ground guides must be used. The rear ground guide must always be visible to the front ground guide.

(8)   If the driver loses sight of the signal, or if there is any question about the signal from the ground guide, the driver should stop until the signal is visible or the confusion is eliminated.

(9)   The front ground guide should immediately signal the driver to stop if he loses sight of the signal of the rear ground guide.

(10)   When a vehicle arrives at a night parking area (other than the occupation of an assembly area as a part of a tactical operation), a ground guide dismounts and establishes contact with the guard on duty. The guide and the driver must understand where the sleeping area is, and where the vehicle is to be parked. The ground guide must search the area for people sleeping on the ground where the vehicle is to park before he moves the vehicle into the parking area. As a minimum, blackout drive must be used. If conditions permit, the service drive should be used.

(11)   All tactical sleeping areas must be marked with a chemical light or flashlight and have a guard equipped with night vision goggles (NVG). The guard must hand carry a flashlight or chemical light to signal or guide vehicles. The guard must be briefed on his duties and on what actions he should take when a vehicle drives into the bivouac or assembly area. A loud, distinct, audible warning device must either be carried by the guard or be accessible in case a vehicle enters a designated sleeping area. Troops who sleep in the area must be briefed on what device is being used and what action they should take. (The unit SOP must specify the same information.) The first priority of the guard is to warn sleeping personnel. He must then attempt to gain the attention of the vehicle driver or vehicle commander without endangering himself.

(12)   All road accesses into the bivouac or assembly area must have a guard posted to warn vehicle crews that there are troops on the ground. The guard should help ground guide the vehicle to its destination, ensuring that, as a minimum, blackout drive is used. If conditions permit, the service drive should be used.

DISABLED VEHICLES

3-29. If a vehicle becomes disabled, the crew should do everything possible not to obstruct traffic or create conditions that might cause an accident. If possible, crew members should move the vehicle out of the way and post guides. Approaching vehicles must be warned. Flares, warning triangles, flashlights, and reflective vests are normally available as warning devices. At least two warning triangles should be carried on each vehicle. To alert traffic to a disabled vehicle, the crew should place the triangles on the shoulder of the road 100 meters behind the vehicle.

ROUGH TERRAIN

3-30. Stryker vehicles travel easily and quickly over rough terrain. This may give drivers false confidence in their driving ability. Frequent accidents occur when Stryker drivers moving cross-country attempt negotiating too quickly obstacles they underestimate or fail to see such as holes and ditches. Accidental steering loss, mechanical failure, and crew casualties can result.

3-31. Drivers can forget that other crew members may not be in secure seating positions, and that they can be thrown around inside of vehicles when encountering rough terrain. The driver and vehicle commander must therefore warn crew members when rough terrain is approaching so they can brace themselves properly. Warnings should also be given when driving under tree limbs and man-made features.

3-32. The difficulty of negotiating rough terrain is compounded when visibility is poor (such as driving through snow, rain, sleet, fog, dust, or battle smoke). Drivers and vehicle commanders must therefore adjust their vehicle speed accordingly to ensure the safety of the crew and vehicle. Reasons drivers lose vehicle control include:

● Loss of steering.
● Loss of brakes.
● Loss of traction.
● Excess speed.

- Over steering.
- Improper braking and downshifting.
- Adverse weather conditions.
- Faulty roadbed.
- Very rough or unstable terrain.

3-33. Drivers and vehicle commanders should observe the following rules when negotiating rough terrain:
- Alert crew members when approaching rough terrain.
- Scan the area ahead of the vehicle to detect obstacles, holes, and ditches as early as possible.
- Use common sense to judge a safe speed to negotiate obstacles, holes, and ditches.
- Make sure all equipment inside the vehicle, especially ammunition and empty canisters, are secured before negotiating rough terrain.
- Make sure crew members and passengers wear installed seatbelts at all times.
- Make sure all hatches are in the locked position before encountering rough terrain. Have crew members periodically inspect open hatches to make sure they stay in the locked positions. Safety pins must be in place if equipped.
- Warn the crew when approaching overhead obstacles.
- Warn the crew when the vehicle goes out of control.

3-34. Unit commanders and vehicle commanders must remember that the urgency of tactical maneuvering does not outweigh the safety of the crew and vehicle. It is the responsibility of the vehicle commander to make sure the driver operates the vehicle at safe speeds to allow control of the vehicle at all times. Safe vehicle operation is directly affected by the terrain and weather conditions.

VEHICLE RECOVERY

3-35. Vehicle recovery is difficult and time consuming. FM 4-30.31 explains in detail the various recovery methods and techniques.

REFUELING OPERATIONS

3-36. Refueling is a total crew effort. Each crew member should be assigned specific duties and responsibilities to complete the process. Drivers normally refuel the vehicle while other crew members take care of the remaining petroleum, oil, and lubricant (POL) requirements. The unit SOP must include the following refueling requirements:
- Any vehicle approaching a refueling point must have two ground guides, one front and one rear. The POL handler may act as ground guide.
- All vehicles should park on level ground with the parking brake on.
- The vehicle engine must be off.
- A crew member or fuel handler on the ground will have a portable fire extinguisher available.
- Vehicles must be grounded while refueling.
- No smoking will be allowed within 50 feet of the vehicle refueling point.
- Any spilled fuel on the vehicle should be cleaned up prior to moving out.
- All POL products stowed on board must be secured prior to moving out.

3-37. During tactical operations, the vehicle may be refueled under combat or simulated combat conditions. Assign each crew member specific duties and responsibilities during refueling. During tactical refueling, the driver remains in the driver's compartment, while the crew refuels the vehicle. Refueling under combat or simulated combat conditions should be the same as under usual conditions except when—
- The vehicle will continue to run.
- The vehicle commander and one crew member refuels the vehicle, while one crew member maintains security.
- A portable fire extinguisher must be held by the second crew member outside the vehicle.

● A fuel handler will be on the ground to supervise the refueling operation. He should have a fire extinguisher available in case of fire, as well.

RAILHEAD OPERATIONS

3-38. A safety briefing should be conducted before railhead operations. The briefing should include the following information:

(1) Do not smoke during loading operations. A smoking area should be designated at least 50 feet away from the nearest vehicle.

(2) Wear protective headgear until you are clear of the railcars.

(3) Be alert for hazards that could cause electrocution. All antennas and equipment stored on the outside of the vehicle should be removed or secured before moving onto the railcar.

(4) Do not stand on top of vehicles.

(5) Secure all weapon systems in travel lock position before loading them onto the railcar.

(6) Do not stand on moving flatcars.

(7) Guide from at least a one-car interval away from the vehicle you are guiding. Ground guides will never guide from the railcars onto which their vehicles are loading.

(8) Do not walk backward while ground guiding on railcars or when you are in the path of a moving vehicle.

(9) Secure all hatches when the rail master has inspected the train and released it for movement.

(10) Loading is complete when the rail master has inspected the train and released it for movement.

NIGHT OPERATIONS

3-39. Night driving operations demand extraordinary precautions by the driver and vehicle commander. They must adjust the speed of the vehicle to ensure the safety of the crew and vehicle.

LIMITED VISIBILITY

● Limited visibility will cause the driver to lose sight of emerging terrain, obstacles, or oncoming traffic. Drivers should not look directly into oncoming headlights due to the possibility of temporary blindness. The driver should watch the right edge of the road until the oncoming vehicle has passed. Once night vision is lost, it takes several minutes to regain it.

● If a life-threatening situation occurs in a training environment during limited visibility or night driving conditions, the vehicle's service driving lights and interior white lights should be turned on (subject to unit policies). This action warns other vehicles of Stryker vehicle presence, indicates there is an emergency, and lets the crew see. Emergency information should be shared by radio on the unit frequency to explain the nature of the problem and the required help. Commanders should specify in the unit SOP that blackout marker or blackout drive (as a minimum) be used during all night maneuvers.

● When driving during limited visibility in a nontactical mode, service drive lights should be turned on. These rules should be in the unit SOP and applied during normal operations. During limited visibility or blackout operations, the unit commander and vehicle crew should ensure the following safety measures are taken:

■ Before moving a vehicle in an assembly area, a member of the crew walks completely around the vehicle to ensure vehicle movement will not endanger anyone. The vehicle commander gives the command "CLEAR" to indicate it is safe to start and move the vehicle.

■ During combined operations, a safe distance is maintained between dismounted troops and moving vehicles.

- Personnel assigned dismounted tasks during blackout conditions are given ample time to complete their tasks. If possible, conduct a detailed daytime reconnaissance of the terrain.
- Individuals assigned dismounted tasks are authorized to halt an exercise to correct a hazardous situation, adjust speed to conditions, or maintain proper interval during convoy operations.
- Vehicle is halted if driver's vision is blocked or VC's vision devices become obscured.

NIGHT VISION DEVICES (NVD)

- Night tactical operations increase the problems facing the driver and vehicle commander. Night vision devices give the driver a limited field of view and distorted depth perception, so vehicle speed must be slower at night than during the day. The vehicle commander should wear NVDs to help his driver negotiate the terrain. During practice sessions, a maximum vehicle speed of 10 mph should be maintained until night vision driving experience is obtained. Avoid overconfidence. NVD skills deteriorate without use, so they must be practiced and maintained. When driving with a NVD, the driver must wear the head harness so both hands remain free for driving. Wearing the NVD for extended periods causes eyestrain, so drivers should stop a minimum of every 30 minutes to rest the eyes for at least 3 minutes.
- During periods of reduced visibility, such as at night during severe weather (especially during heavy rain, frequent lightning flashes, or heavy overcast), the night vision viewer cannot be relied upon for safe vehicle operations. The unit SOP should specify whether or not to slow down or stop field exercises when severe environmental hazards exist.

DUST AND SMOKE

3-40. During normal operations, dust can be a concern when driving in any formation; smoke will most likely present a problem during field training exercises. Drivers and vehicle commanders should observe the following rules when traveling under dust or smoke conditions:

(1) Regardless of visibility conditions, goggles should be worn when driving in an open-hatch position. Clear-lensed goggles should be worn at night unless NVDs are used. Bandannas or surgical masks should be worn over the nose and mouth to avoid breathing heavy dust or smoke.

(2) Vehicles in an extended convoy should maintain a distance of twice the normal interval, or as specified in the unit SOP, during dusty conditions to allow the dust to dissipate. When driving on extremely dusty roads or trails, a staggered column formation should be used if traffic conditions permit. If vehicles in a convoy become engulfed in dust, the convoy commander should adjust his convoy's speed accordingly. Any vehicle commander who becomes engulfed in dust should alert the convoy commander by radio, move to the right side of the road, and stop to allow the dust to dissipate. Do not back up vehicles while engulfed in dust. Observe extreme caution to ensure oncoming vehicles are not jeopardized. The lead vehicle must warn trail vehicles to return to column formation if traffic is encountered.

(3) While driving in-line, vehicles should maintain their horizontal distance and adjust speed to dust or smoke conditions. If dust or smoke becomes so thick that total disorientation or vertigo occur, the platoon leader/sergeant should radio to halt the formation. Vehicles should not be backed up while engulfed in dust or smoke.

SHALLOW WATER FORDING OPERATIONS

3-41. A preoperational plan with an emphasis on safety is the key to reducing unnecessary risks. Following are some important shallow water fording considerations that should be incorporated into the unit SOP:

(1) Make sure the fording site has adequate entrance and exit points and a firm bottom.

(2) Make sure the water depth at the fording site is below the vehicle fording limits and the site is clear of submerged obstacles.

(3) Make sure dismounted troops crossing are attached to a safety line.

(4) Do not cross more than one vehicle at the same time, and do not cross a vehicle beside dismounted troops.

(5) During training exercises, make sure drivers and crew members wear life vests if water is over 4-feet deep.

(6) Do not exceed 4 mph.

(7) Make sure all vehicle fording and swimming instructions are followed in accordance with the vehicle TM.

(8) Do not wear load-bearing equipment (LBE) during fording operations. It could snag on vehicle components and prevent crew members from evacuating through the top hatches during emergencies.

(9) Leave top hatches open in case the crew needs to evacuate.

(10) Store sensitive items and small arms inside the vehicle. If the vehicle sinks, these items can be recovered easily.

COLD WEATHER OPERATIONS

3-42. Cold weather conditions require additional precautions and actions by the driver. The driver must adjust speed, following distance, and driving techniques to counter the hazards of snow, ice, and freezing conditions. The unit SOP should list winter clothing that will be carried by crews during cold weather operations. Squad leaders should inspect crew members to make sure the required clothing is worn during maneuvers and while conducting vehicle maintenance.

CONVOY DRIVING

3-43. The planning and coordination involved in convoy operations require aggressive staff action. FM 55-30, chapter 5 describes convoy operations, telling how to plan, organize, and control them, and provides a guide for training individual drivers.

FORCE PROTECTION (FRATRICIDE)

3-44. Fratricide is a component of force protection and is closely related to safety.

(1) Fratricide is the employment of weapons with the intent to kill the enemy or destroy his equipment that results in unforeseen and unintentional death, injury, or damage to friendly personnel or equipment.

(2) Fratricide is by definition an accident.

(3) Risk assessment and management is the mechanism with which incidence of fratricide can be controlled.

PRIMARY CAUSES

3-45. The primary causes of fratricide are:

- *Direct fire control failures.* These occur when units fail to develop defensive and, particularly, offensive fire control plans.

- *Land navigation failures.* This results when units stray out of sector, report wrong locations, and become disoriented.

- *Combat identification failures.* These failures include gunners being unable to distinguish thermal and optical signatures near the maximum range of their sighting systems and units in proximity mistaking each other for the enemy under limited visibility conditions.

- *Inadequate control measures.* Units fail to disseminate the minimum maneuver and fire support control measures necessary to tie control measures to recognizable terrain or events.

- *Reporting communication failures.* Units at all levels face problems in generating timely, accurate, and complete reports as locations and tactical situations change.
- *Weapons errors.* Lapses in individual discipline lead to weapon charging errors, accidental discharges, mistakes with explosives and hand grenades, and similar incidents.

HARMFUL RESULTS

3-46. Fratricide results in unacceptable losses and increases the risk of mission failure. Fratricide undermines the unit's ability to survive and function. Units experiencing fratricide often observe these consequences:

- Loss of confidence in the unit leadership.
- Increasing self-doubt among leaders.
- Hesitation to use supporting combat systems.
- Over supervision of units.
- Hesitation to conduct night operations.
- Loss of aggressiveness during fire and maneuver.
- Loss of initiative.
- Disrupted operations.
- General degradation of cohesiveness, morale, and combat power.

3-47. Actions to control fratricide should include the following:

- Establish a restricted fire line or other spatial separation from supporting fires.
- Reconnoiter and mark the entire route with key leaders.
- Train vehicle recognition and identification continually.
- Complete full-force rehearsals of all phases and possible contingencies.
- Coordinate with any adjacent units that will move mounted or dismounted.
- Enforce absolute compliance with sleep plan.

NOTE: Fratricide risk assessment and reduction measures are provided in the Center for Army Lessons Learned (CALL) Handbook No. 92-3. To obtain this handbook, contact the Center for Army Lessons Learned, US Army Combined Arms Command, ATTN: ATZL-CTL, Fort Leavenworth, KS 66027-7000. (E-mail address: call@leav-emh1.army mil)

This page intentionally left blank.

Chapter 4

Environmental Awareness

Protection of natural resources is an ever-increasing Army concern. It is the responsibility of all unit leaders to decrease, and if possible, eliminate damage to the environment when conducting training, operations other than war, and (as appropriate) during combat. Instructors should reconnoiter potential driving course sites to make sure vehicle maneuver minimizes damages to vegetation and waterways. This chapter focuses on the importance of environmental awareness and resource responsibilities in Stryker maneuver areas.

ENVIRONMENTAL RISK MANAGEMENT

4-1. Environmental risk management consists of the following steps.

IDENTIFY HAZARDS

4-2. Identify potential sources for environmental degradation during analysis of mission, enemy, terrain and weather, troops and support available, time available, civil considerations (METT-TC) factors. This requires identification of environmental hazards. An environmental hazard is a condition with the potential for polluting air, soil, or water, and destroying significant natural or cultural resources.

ASSESS HAZARDS

4-3. Analyze potential severity of environmental degradation using environmental risk assessment matrixes (Figure 4-1). Severity of environmental degradation must be considered when determining the potential effect of an operation on the environment. The risk impact value is defined as an indicator of the severity of environmental degradation. Quantify the risk to the environment resulting from the operation as extremely high, medium, or low. Any environmental risk impact value should be determined conservatively. Consult with the environmental office for other local requirements relating to wildlife and natural vegetation.

MAKE ENVIRONMENTAL RISK DECISIONS

4-4. Make decisions by analyzing the environmental risk assessment matrix. Determine if alternate actions will better protect the environment while still accomplishing the mission. Determine if the mission needs to be adjusted by the commander.

BRIEF CHAIN OF COMMAND

4-5. Brief the chain of command (including the installation environmental office [if applicable]) on proposed plans and pertinent high-risk environmental matrixes. Risk decisions are made at a level of command that corresponds to the degree of risk. Gather the appropriate land-use and digging permits.

IMPLEMENT CONTROLS

4-6. Implement environmental protection measures by integrating them into plans, orders, packing lists, SOPs, training performance standards, and rehearsals.

SUPERVISE

4-7.   Supervise and enforce environmental protection standards.

> **NOTE:** Each U.S. installation is subject to local and state environmental regulations in addition to federal legislation. For information specific to your activity, contact the installation environmental office. (If you are overseas or on deployment, contact your higher S-3/G-3.)

ENVIRONMENTAL RISK ASSESSMENT MATRIX

4-8.   The following steps describe how to develop an environmental risk assessment matrix:

- Complete an Environmental Risk Assessment Worksheet for each environmental area requiring assessment. For example, the top section of the example worksheet (Figure 4-1) addresses the environmental area of water pollution.
  (1) In the column labeled **Unit Operations**, list every operation or major task Soldiers will perform during training.
  (2) Under **Risk Impact,** rate each unit operation or major task on a 0-5 scale. Rate "0" as causing minimal risk impact on the environment, and "5" if major environmental impact is expected. In Figure 4-1, the appropriate rating for each unit operation has been highlighted in gray.
- Complete the Overall Risk Assessment Form (see example middle Figure 4-1).
  (1) List all the environmental areas (such as water pollution) in the first column.
  (2) List all unit operations in the next columns, saving the last column for a total *risk rating* of each environmental area.
  (3) Copy from the Environmental Risk Assessment Worksheet into this form section the assessed risk impact rating for each environmental area. For example, in Figure 4-1, **Movement of Heavy Vehicles/Supplies,** was rated a "5" on the worksheet for water pollution. That rating has been copied into the Overall Risk Assessment Form where the environmental area **Water Pollution** intersects with the unit operation **Movement of Heavy Vehicles/Systems**.
  (4) Add all the risk impact ratings for each environmental area and write that number in the last column labeled **Risk Rating**. The total risk rating for **Water Pollution** is 12.
  (5) After the risk rating for each environmental area has been computed, add all the risk ratings to get an overall rating. In the worksheet example, the overall rating for training is 43.

4-9.   Compare the overall rating with the point totals in the Risk Categories section of the assessment form (see example bottom Figure 4-1). If the risk assessment score applied to the matrix falls into the low or medium risk categories, Stryker training can proceed with minimal environmental risk. If risk category is "high" or "extremely high," the environmental assessor's chain of command should be notified.

Environmental Area: Water Pollution				Rating: 12	
Unit Operations	**Risk Impact**				
Movement of heavy vehicles/supplies	5	4	3	2	1	0
Movement of personnel and light vehicles/systems	5	4	3	2	1	0
Assembly area procedures	5	4	3	2	1	0
Field maintenance of equipment	5	4	3	2	1	0
Garrison maintenance of equipment	5	4	3	2	1	0

Environmental Risk Assessment Worksheet

THIS ASSESSMENT IS DONE FOR EACH CATEGORY

	Movement of heavy vehicles/systems	Movement of personnel and light vehicles/systems	Assembly area procedures	Field maintenance of equipment	Garrison maintenance of equipment	Risk rating
Air pollution	2	1	0	1	0	4
Archaeological and historical sites	3	3	0	1	0	7
Hazardous material/waste	2	1	1	2	0	6
Noise pollution	1	0	1	0	0	2
Threatened/endangered species	1	1	0	0	0	2
Water pollution	5	2	3	2	0	12
Wetland protection	5	5	1	2	0	10
Overall rating	19	10	6	8	0	43

Overall Environmental Risk Assessment Form

Category	Range	Environmental Damage	Decision Maker
Low	0-58	Little or none	Appropriate level
Medium	59-117	Minor	Appropriate level
High	118-149	Significant	Division Cdr
Extremely High	150-175	Severe	MACOM Cdr

Risk Categories

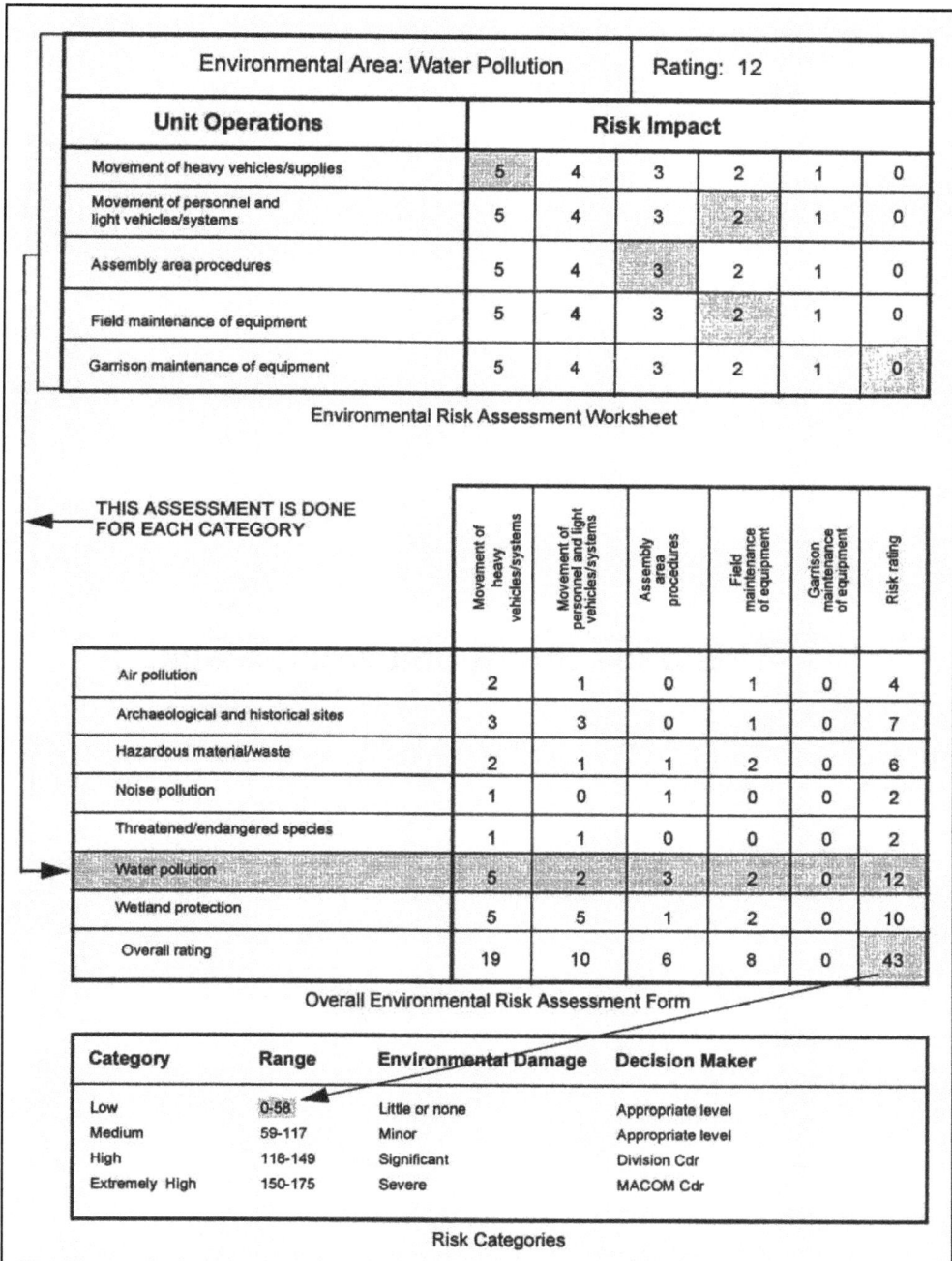

Figure 4-1. Environmental risk assessment worksheet (example).

This page intentionally left blank.

Chapter 5

How to Use Training Support Packages

Training support packages (TSPs) are complete, exportable teaching packages that integrate training products, materials, and information necessary to train one or more critical tasks. The purpose of this chapter is to explain the proper use and acquisition of the Stryker vehicle driver training TSPs referenced in this publication.

OVERVIEW

5-1. TRADOC Regulation 350-70, Systems Approach to Training Management, Processes, and Products, Appendix E (9 March 1999), defines the contents and format of a TSP. The TSPs referenced in this publication prescribe "model" Stryker vehicle training programs for units. Unit commanders have authority to make any minor modifications necessary to conform to unit training restrictions. However, the TSP proponent must approve major modifications.

HOW TO USE STRYKER DRIVER TSPs

5-2. In 2005 the Commander, TRADOC, directed the U.S. Army Infantry School to design a Stryker vehicle driver training program with developed TSPs that would standardize Stryker driver training Armywide. The Stryker vehicle driver TSPs that can be accessed through the process described at the end of this chapter (paragraph 5-14) were developed for this program. These TSPs can be used with flexible training programs as stand-alone courses, or as integrated additions to existing training. Each has been designed to provide units with driver training materials that promote safe driving practices, accident avoidance, and technical competence.

CONTENTS OF A TSP

5-3. Each Stryker vehicle TSP contains the following:

Title Page

5-4. The title page contains general information such as the TSP number, title, individual tasks addressed, effective date, proponent, and address for sending comments and recommendations.

Preface

5-5. The preface contains the conditions and standards for all tasks covered in the TSP as well as a table of contents. It also specifies if the TSP includes more than one lesson.

Lesson(s)

5-6. Each lesson consists of five sections. Examples follow.

TSP EXAMPLE

SECTION I - ADMINISTRATIVE DATA

5-7. This section contains information needed to manage training, including the following:

- **All Courses Including this Lesson.** The lesson plan(s) contained in the TSP may also be taught as part of a residential course or contained in another exportable training program. Some lessons are simply taught as part of unit training.
- **Task(s) Taught or Supported.** If the TSP contains only one lesson, the tasks listed here will be the same as the ones listed in the preface.
- **Reinforced Task(s).** These tasks are not taught as part of the TSP. However, the TSP provides refresher or integrated training.
- **Academic Hours.** This paragraph specifies the time required to train each task, administer each lesson (if more than one), and conduct student testing. It also specifies an overall time for implementing the TSP.
- **Test Lesson Number.** If the test is not included in this lesson, list the test lesson number in which this lesson's terminal learning objective is tested and the test results are reviewed with the students. Put "N/A" if not tested in a separate lesson.
- **Prerequisite Lesson(s).** Some TSPs or lessons within a TSP may build on the contents of other ones. In such cases, this paragraph lists TSPs or lesson plans in the recommended training sequence.
- **Security Clearance/Access.** Most TSPs will be unclassified. Any statement that limits distribution will be listed here.
- **Foreign Disclosure Restrictions.** List the appropriate foreign disclosure restriction statement. Refer to TR 350-70 Chapter I-1 for foreign disclosure restriction statements.
- **References.** This paragraph lists references used to develop the TSP. It may differ from the training materials required by the instructor and the students.
- **Student Study Assignments.** The instructor may require students to study material prior to implementation of the TSP. In such cases, the instructor needs to prepare a student handout describing the study assignment and make provisions for students to pick up study materials.
- **Instructor Requirements.** This paragraph specifies the number of instructors, to include whether a primary instructor and small group instructors are needed. It also describes any special qualifications instructors must possess to train the task(s) to standard.
- **Additional Support Personnel Requirements.** This paragraph lists support personnel and their qualification requirements. Support personnel could include bus drivers, audiovisual equipment operators, and range operators.
- **Equipment Required.** This paragraph lists all equipment and tools needed to accomplish instruction. Examples include the number and type of Stryker vehicles, night vision devices, protective masks, and dummy mines.
- **Materials Required.** Instructor materials include manuals, checklists, terrain boards, audiovisual supplies, and other instructional aids. Student materials include anything students need before or during the class such as maps, compasses, and flashlights.
- **Classroom, Training Area, and Range Requirements.** For exportable TSPs, these requirements may be general in nature since they are dependent on unit resources.
- **Ammunition Requirements.** This paragraph lists all ammunition requirements using official nomenclature and approved basis of issue. (The TSPs in this publication do not require the use of ammunition.)
- **Instructional Guidance.** This paragraph describes what the instructor needs to accomplish prior to training. It may include information about scheduling resources, preparing other instructors, and preparing the training site.
- **Branch Safety Manager Approval.** If not required, put N/A. See chapter I-2 of TR 350-70 for requirements.
- **Proponent Lesson Plan Approvals.** The lesson plans in this publication's TSPs have been approved by the Chief of the Staff of the Army and by the schools proponent for each Stryker vehicle. Any significant changes cannot be implemented without coordination with the proponent.

SECTION II - INTRODUCTION

5-8.   This section specifies the method of instruction for the TSP or lesson, the instructor-to-student ratio, the time required to teach the lesson, and the media used (if applicable). It also contains the following:

- **Motivator.** This short motivational introduction to the lesson can be a discussion, short demonstration, or videotape designed to peak the student's interest and to focus them on the material they are about to learn.
- **Terminal Learning Objective.** This objective describes what the student will be able to do at the completion of the lesson. It specifies an action, conditions, and an overall standard.
- **Safety Requirements.** This paragraph describes the general safety requirements for the lesson, including potential hazards. Warnings and cautions should be listed in the presentation section of the lesson (since they will be more meaningful to students when presented in the context of job performance).
- **Risk Assessment Level.** The TSP will list an initial risk assessment of low, medium, caution, or high. Ratings are assigned by TSP proponents based on analysis of potential hazards that could be encountered during training. A hazard is defined as any condition with the potential to cause injury to personnel, damage to equipment, or loss of materiel. Training with a risk assessment of "high" must be approved by the unit or installation commander.
- **Environmental Considerations.** This paragraph describes how to ensure the training does not have an adverse impact on the environment. It does not address how the environment affects task performance.
- **Evaluation.** This paragraph describes how the terminal learning objective will be tested, and the minimum passing score.
- **Instructional Lead-in.** The purpose of the instructional lead-in is to tie the terminal learning objective to previous learning or student experience and lead into the actual presentation.

SECTION III - PRESENTATION

5-9.   This section describes the instructional methods and content. It consists of the following:

- **Enabling Learning Objective.** The enabling learning objective specifies the action, conditions, and standards for a task or part of a task. Some TSPs may not have enabling learning objectives.
- **Learning Steps/Activities.** For each learning step/activity, the TSP will list the method of instruction, instructor-to-student ratio, time of instruction, and media (if required). If this information remains the same for a large number of learning steps/activities, it may be listed following the enabling learning objective prior to the first learning step/activity.
- **Notes.** The lesson may include notes throughout the learning steps/activities to remind instructors to check on student learning and ask questions.

SECTION IV - SUMMARY

5-10. This section provides guidance on summarizing instruction and soliciting student feedback prior to testing. It consists of the following:

- **Review/Summarize Lesson.** This paragraph provides a brief summary of the material covered in the lesson or TSP.
- **Check on Learning.** This paragraph includes specific questions that the instructor can use to determine the students' mastery of the lesson or TSP.
- **Transition to Next Lesson.** This paragraph explains how the next lesson relates to this one. This paragraph may be deleted if there is not a follow-on lesson.

SECTION V - STUDENT EVALUATION

5-11. This section describes how students will be evaluated and how they will receive feedback. It consists of the following:

- **Testing Requirements.** This paragraph describes the testing method and pass/fail criteria. It includes a full description of the test administrative procedures, to include setting up the test site, providing instructions to students, and using a scoring checklist.
- **Feedback Requirements.** This paragraph describes how students can learn their test scores and schedule remedial/refresher training.

Tests

5-12. Each TSP contains a written test and one or more hands-on tests. Each test consists of a test administration guide, an answer key (or test scoring checklist), and an evaluation feedback statement that tells the students how to get remedial training if required. The test administration guide provides the following information:

- Task number and title.
- Personnel, equipment, and material required.
- Test planning time.
- Site requirements (and a layout diagram if appropriate).
- Pretest preparation.
- Instructions for administering the test and instructions for scoring the test. The scoring checklist contains instructions to the students and the performance measures evaluated by the instructor.

Supporting Materials

5-13. Some TSPs may contain viewgraphs or student handouts that enhance the instruction.

HOW TO OBTAIN COPIES OF STRYKER VEHICLE DRIVER TSPS

5-14. Stryker Driver TSPs are provided to unit S3s as a stay-behind package upon completion of Stryker New Equipment Training (NET). When evolving equipment changes or modifications occur, units are provided updated instruction versions in the form of errata sheets. Contact your battalion master driver or S3 for the latest TSP versions.

Chapter 6

STRYKER DRIVER VISION ENHANCER AN/VAS-5

Stryker vehicle drivers play a major roll in unit success. To remain combat effective, they must be technically and tactically proficient. To accommodate this, Stryker drivers are trained day and night to operate vehicles in open terrain, on roadways, and in traffic. Stryker vehicle drivers are trained to use the driver vision enhancer (DVE). This chapter explains improvements made to the DVE, introduces new DVE technology, and discusses the modes in which a Stryker DVE can be employed.

SECTION I — CHARACTERISTICS AND CAPABILITIES

INTRODUCTION

6-1.   SBCT Soldiers and Stryker crews operate in Iraq around the clock battling enemy forces and the environment in ever-changing hostile conditions. In some instances Stryker crews are forced to operate "buckled-up" (hatches closed) for protection against top attacks when traveling through urban areas. Sniper fire and other threats that affect Soldier and equipment alike are a constant danger. These situations require disciplined Stryker crews who know how to operate with hatches closed. Vision restricted conditions require periscope and video display screen skills that allow day and night maneuver over and around unknown terrain. This section addresses these conditions directly and includes recommended techniques and procedures employed to lessen any apprehension a crew may have when maneuvering "buckled-up".

CAPABILITIES

6-2.   The driver vision enhancer (DVE) is a compact, lightweight, uncooled, passive, thermal imaging system designed for use on a variety of combat and tactical wheeled vehicles during darkness or periods of degraded visibility. Battlefield conditions such as smoke, dust, haze, fog, and rain will produce these poor visibility conditions. Under clear atmospheric conditions, the DVE will detect a standing person or a 22-inch (55.9-centimeter) object at a distance of at least 360 feet (110 meters).

6-3.   The AN/VAS-5 Stryker DVE provides Stryker drivers with:

- Increased fields-of-view during day/night battle conditions; hatches closed and secured.
- Depth perception.
- Vehicle situational awareness.
- Imagery definition.
- Distance.
- Capability to see during darkness and periods of degraded visibility
- Ability to drive in smoke, dust, haze, and some weather related conditions.
- Ability to drive without emitting visible light or other traceable signal.

NOTE: During periods of degraded visibility or under conditions of low thermal contrast, drivers must use caution and reduce vehicle speed accordingly. A displayed infrared (IR) scene is two-dimensional and does not convey depth perception.

ENVIRONMENTAL CHARACTERISTICS

6-4. The DVE withstands shock or vibration received during normal use, handling, or transportation with no performance degradation, including:

- Ambient Temperature:
  - Operating temperature from 120.2 °F (49 °C) to -34.6 °F (-37 °C).
  - Storage temperature from 159.8 °F (71 °C) to -50.8 °F (-46 °C).
- Humidity:
  - The DVE is not affected by external humidity conditions.
- Corrosion:
  - The sensor, display control module, and vehicle adapter are composed of an aluminum alloy that usually does not corrode.
- Altitude:
  - The DVE is operable with no performance degradation at altitudes up to 15,000 feet (4.6 kilometers).

OPERATIONAL FEATURES

6-5. AN/VAS-5A DVE equipped Stryker vehicle drivers experience increased maneuver ability while maintaining situational awareness with improvements in field of view (FOV), depth perception, and imagery definition.

START UP TIME

- Within 3 minutes at: -1 °F TO +120 °F (17 °C TO +49 °C).
- Up to 5 minutes at: -35 °F TO -1 °F (37 °C TO -17 °C)

FIELD OF VIEW (FOV):

- 30 degrees in elevation by 40 degrees in Azimuth.

Target detection

- Under clear atmospheric conditions can detect a person or a 22 inch object at a distance of 360 feet (110 meters) or more.

FOCUS

- 5 meters to infinity.

INFRARED SIGNATURES

- Only collects IR energy from field of view.

VISIBLE LIGHT

- Ignores visible light input.
- Allows only IR imagery to be seen by operator.

VERSATILITY

- Effective 24 hours a day.
- Enhances vision during poor visibility conditions.
- Able to see camouflaged objects.

OPERATING TEMPERATURE

- +120.2 °F TO -34.6 °F (+49 °C TO -37 °C).

DVE OPTIMIZATION GOALS

- First – Discriminating an object from the field of view background.
- Second – Determining whether the detected object is a hazard, safe path, or obstacle.
  - Cliff
  - Road
  - Boulder
- Third – Negotiating a path around the obstacle.

> **WARNING**
>
> When the DVE is operated in dense fog, IR smoke, or heavy rains, objects may not be readily detectable. If an object has exactly the same temperature as surrounding objects, it may not be readily detectable. Infrared energy cannot be detected through most glass. Operators must therefore maintain an awareness of environmental/weather conditions, and adjust speeds to suit the prevailing operating environment and terrain.

VISUAL VS. VIDEO/THERMAL IMAGES

6-6. Any video image is less clear than a direct visual image. Thermal system images are even less clear.

- In black and white visual images, shades of gray represent brightness of colors.
- In DVE thermal images, shades of gray represent intensity of IR energy.

6-7. Objects that are bright visually are not necessarily bright in thermal imagery. Visual brightness depends on color, visual reflectance of object, and intensity of visual light sources. Distance affects intensity:

- 500 meters: reference
- 1000 meters: 1/4 as intense
- 1500 meters: 1/9 as intense
- 2000 meters: 1/16 as intense

6-8. Thermal image brightness depends mainly on—

- Temperature and emissivity of object (emissivity: rate that material discharges IR energy).
- Intensity and duration of energy sources affecting temperature of object.
- Level, gain, brightness, and polarity settings.

6-9. Glass (windows, headlights) attenuates IR energy and will look cool unless heated or reflecting IR energy of higher intensity. Shadowing in IR images may not be noticeable unless objects have been stationary long enough for the surface to change temperature.

NOTE: Interpretation of thermal image comes with experience and practice.

THERMAL SIGNATURES

6-10. Man-made objects present identifiable thermal signatures because they are different from the natural environment. Objects include:

- Roads and tracks.
- Fences and obstacles.

6-11. Combustion, friction, and body heat provide thermal signatures for mechanical and living objects such as:

- Vehicles (tracks, tires, engines, shock absorbers).
- People and animals.

CONCERNS

6-12. Geometric and physical conditions can make distinguishing objects in thermal scenes more difficult. Control settings affect image quality. Therefore, time is critical. When conditions obscure thermal scenes drivers should avoid unnecessary adjustments of controls, stop the vehicle, select close and far objects, and adjust DVE controls.

STRYKER WITH AN/VAS-5A (V) DISPLAY MODULE

6-13. The AN/VAS-5 DVE (Figure 6-1) consists of two major assemblies: a display control module (1); and a sensor assembly (2). Mounting of the sensor assembly is based on vehicle designs that provide the greatest amount of operator vision. The unit's improved sensor electronics addresses "thermal wash-out". Stryker DVE sensors are mounted front-center (3) for optimum viewing as shown in Figure 6-2.

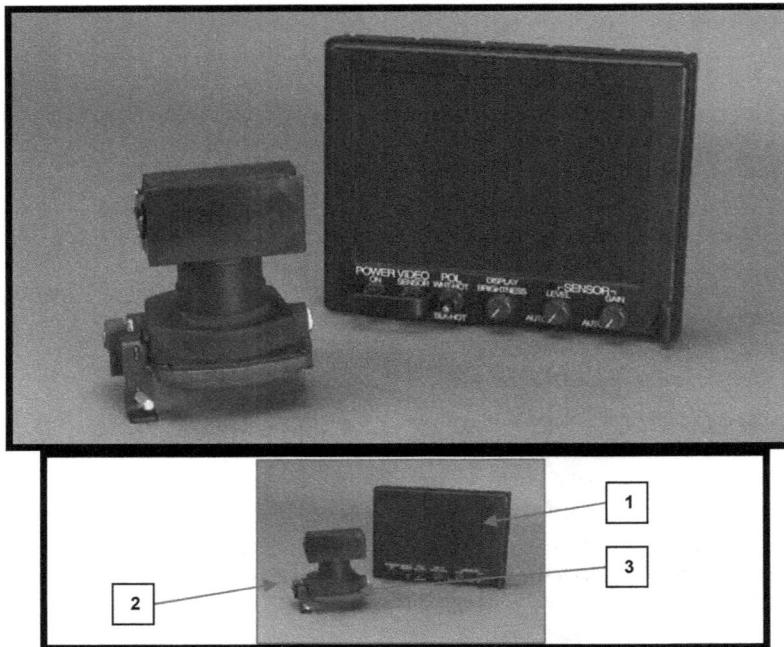

Figure 6-1. Sensor modules.

Figure 6-2. DVE sensor location.

NOTE: DVE sensors cannot pan or tilt because they are fix mounted.

DRIVER VISION ENHANCER (DVE) VIEWING

6-14. *Passive night vision* devices capture emitted light. *Thermal* devices capture emitted heat. Thermal imagery is affected by ambient temperatures produced by terrain and man-made objects. Trees, brush, rock, and man-made objects (dwellings, metal material) absorb daytime heat, releasing it after sunset. Large flat surface areas heated by the sun dissipate much faster than natural or man-made objects, releasing their stored heat gradually. Some objects hold heat much longer than others. Rocks for instance, take longer to cool than a tree or a metal object. The more mass, the longer it takes to cool. Weather conditions such as rain, fog, and cold air can also reduce thermal energies.

DVE Appearance

6-15. Objects appear black on the DVE display, making it difficult to determine type, size, and depth.

6-16. To compensate for thermal neutral conditions, drivers can activate the display control module to high gain mode.

6-17. In DVE thermal images (Figures 6-3 through 6-7), shades of gray represent intensity of IR energy. Thermal image brightness depends mainly on:
- Temperature and emissivity of object.
- Intensity and duration of energy sources affecting temperature of object.
- Contrast, brightness, and polarity settings.

NOTE: Although actual photographs are not the thermal images shown in figures 6-3 through 6-7, they do offer a comparison of real time vs. projected thermal images as seen by the driver.

6-18. Figure 6-3 illustrates visual vs. thermal discrimination of natural objects.

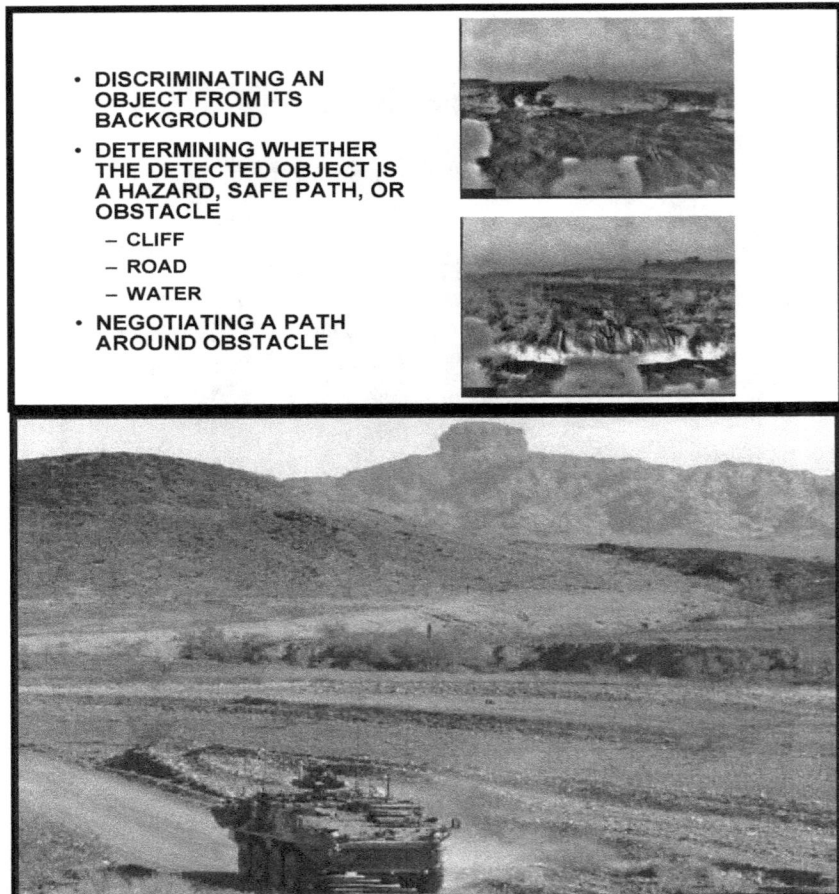

- DISCRIMINATING AN OBJECT FROM ITS BACKGROUND
- DETERMINING WHETHER THE DETECTED OBJECT IS A HAZARD, SAFE PATH, OR OBSTACLE
  - CLIFF
  - ROAD
  - WATER
- NEGOTIATING A PATH AROUND OBSTACLE

Figure 6-3. Visual vs. DVE thermal discrimination of natural objects.

6-19. Figure 6-4 illustrates visual vs. thermal discrimination of man-made objects.

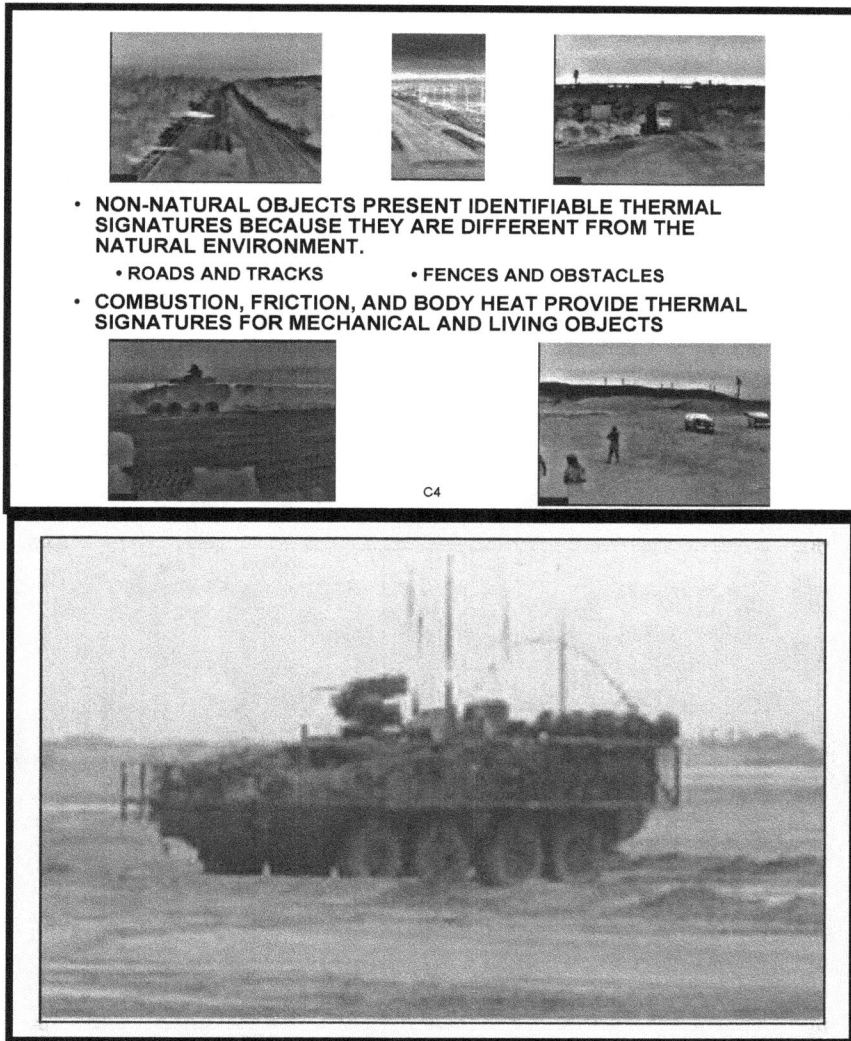

- NON-NATURAL OBJECTS PRESENT IDENTIFIABLE THERMAL SIGNATURES BECAUSE THEY ARE DIFFERENT FROM THE NATURAL ENVIRONMENT.
  - ROADS AND TRACKS
  - FENCES AND OBSTACLES
- COMBUSTION, FRICTION, AND BODY HEAT PROVIDE THERMAL SIGNATURES FOR MECHANICAL AND LIVING OBJECTS

C4

Figure 6-4. Visual vs. thermal discrimination of man-made objects.

6-20. Figure 6-5 illustrates distance vs. thermal intensity.

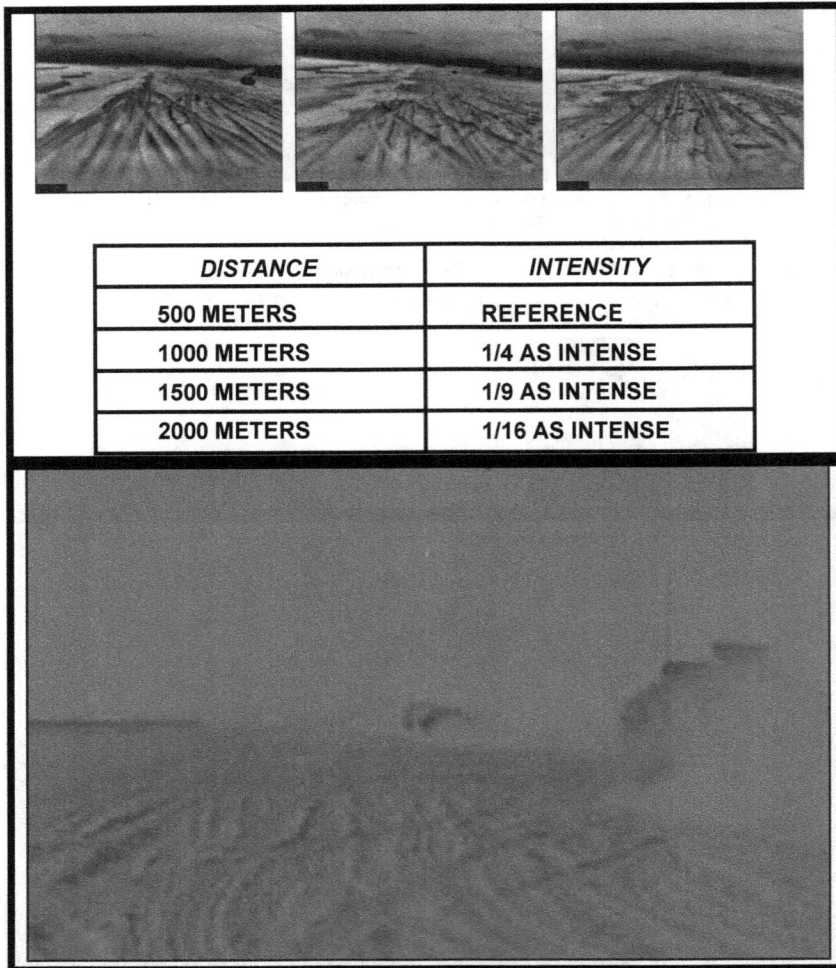

DISTANCE	INTENSITY
500 METERS	REFERENCE
1000 METERS	1/4 AS INTENSE
1500 METERS	1/9 AS INTENSE
2000 METERS	1/16 AS INTENSE

Figure 6-5. Distance vs. thermal intensity.

6-21. Figure 6-6 illustrates visual vs. thermal viewing angle intensity.

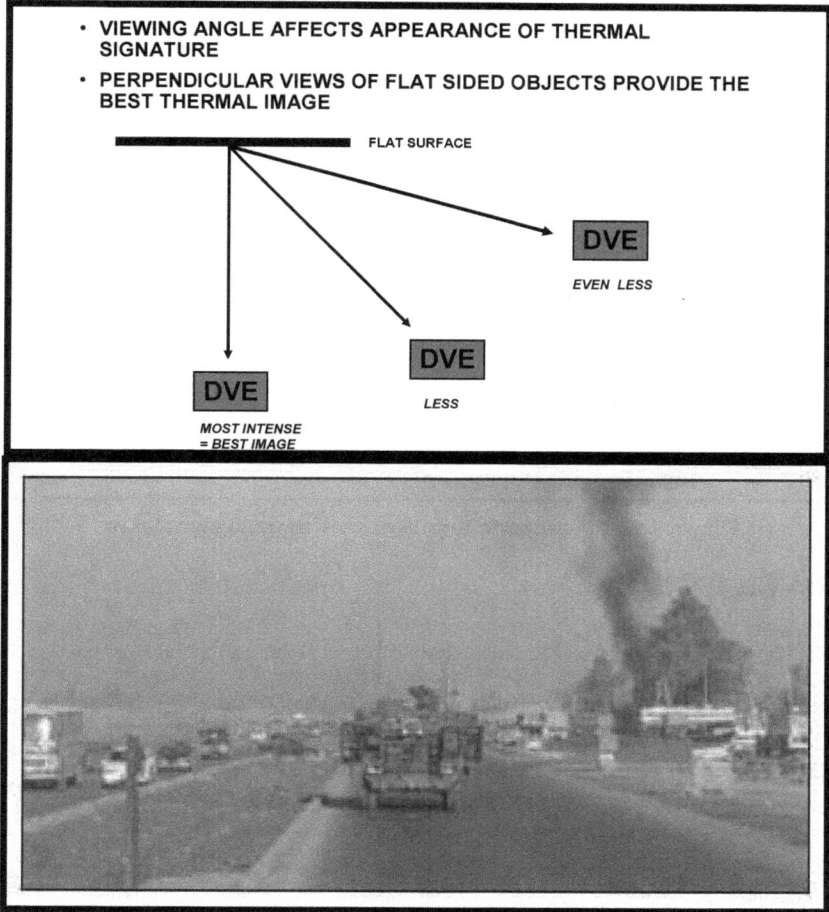

Figure 6-6. Visual vs. thermal viewing angle intensity.

6-22. Figure 6-7 illustrates atmospheric turbulence vs. thermal signatures.

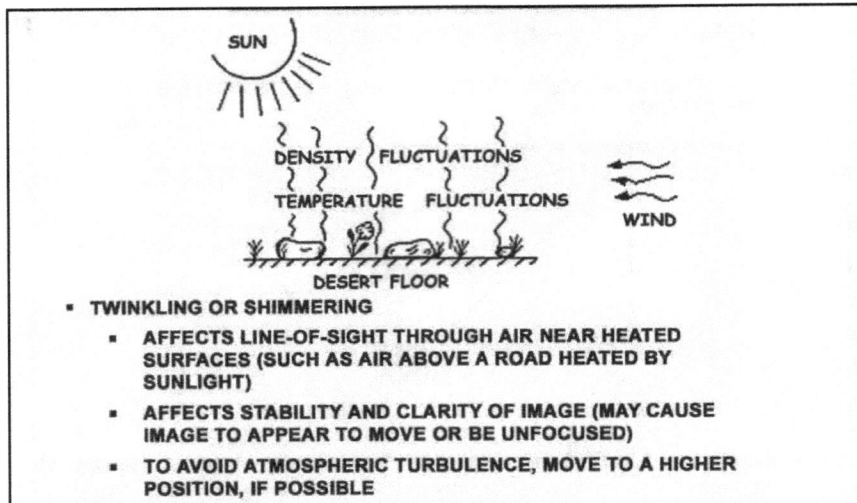

Figure 6-7. Atmospheric turbulence vs. thermal signatures.

CROSSOVER PERIODS

6-23. There are two short periods each day called "crossover periods" when most natural objects are essentially the same temperature: when they cool down at night, and when they heat up in the early morning. Since objects are near the same temperature during these periods, the image display quality is degraded because there is not much temperature difference the DVE can distinguish. This also happens when a heavy rain makes all natural objects close to the same temperature.

6-24. Crossover periods are a daily cycle in which objects are heated by sun then cool down at night.
- **Sunrise:** Objects begin to absorb thermal energy and increase in temperature.
- **Sunset:** Objects begin to lose thermal energy and decrease in temperature.

6-25. Motionless objects or things not generating their own thermal energy approach the same temperature. Such objects include:
- Large dense objects (stationary vehicles) heat and cool slowly.
- Lightweight objects (foliage) heat and cool quickly.
- Heavy objects that have high thermal mass.
- Lightweight objects that have low thermal mass.

6-26. An overcast sky reduces solar energy absorbed by objects. Surface temperatures under this condition tend to become equal, causing reduced contrast particulates (dust, haze, smog, smoke). This degrades DVE imagery. How much degradation occurs depends on size, type, and concentration of particles.

6-27. High humidity produces surface reflections that can cause deceptive imagery. Example: Smooth, glossy surfaces (windows, mirrors, still water) can produce strong reflections of IR light from other sources. This is generally not a problem, but if occurs it can be deceiving.

OPERATIONAL CONSIDERATIONS

6-28. Time is critical on a battlefield, so training and practice is important. Well-trained drivers can avoid any unnecessary trial and error adjusting of controls when the enemy is near. Wet weather also has a significant effect on DVE thermal imagery. It cools down objects, creates fog or clouds, and degrades IR energy. "Thermal washout" can occur during periods of heavy rain. All terrain features, natural and man-made, approach the same temperature (thermal neutral conditions) during heavy rains, affecting DVE thermal images in the following ways:

- Light rain   → Slight degradation
- Medium rain   → Medium degradation
- Cloudburst   → Heavy degradation
- Long duration rain storms   → Heavy degradation
    - All objects approach the same temperature creating thermal neutral conditions

NOTE: Thermal imagers are slightly better than visual optics during wet weather conditions. DVE high gain feature improves thermal image in these conditions.

SECTION II — TACTICS, TECHNIQUES, AND PROCEDURES

DRIVER TACTICS, TECHNIQUES, AND PROCEDURES

6-29. "Drivers must be tactically and technically proficient" was a valuable lesson learned (and relearned) by maneuvering commanders in the beginning of Operation Iraqi Freedom. Drivers involved in convoy operations must constantly remain alert for ambushes, maneuver tactically to support by fire, and at times, use their vehicles as shields to protect ground warriors. Most driver training beyond basic driving skills consists of on the job training experience. But lessons learned yesterday give us an edge in training today.

6-30. Driver training should progress from basic to advanced stages.
- Basic skills consist of maneuvering from an open hatch position, on and off road, during normal conditions.
- Advance skills consist of maneuvering with hatch closed, navigating using the DVE, on and off road, during day/night conditions.

NOTE: Leaders should take advantage of inclement weather conditions to acclimate drivers.

6-31. Driving a Stryker "buttoned-up" while depending on the DVE for navigation can be a discriminator in driver selection. Not everyone can do it. Some Soldiers become claustrophobic; others become indecisive. Therefore, testing Soldier ability to adapt to enclosed navigation conditions while using the DVE should be conducted as part of basic driver training.

NOTE: For safety purposes, "buttoned-up" DVE training should be performed in a controlled environment.

6-32. Advanced training should include:
- Driving cross-country, day and night. Drivers can recognize and navigate terrain features, and select routes that offer cover and concealment.
- Driving in traffic, day and night. Driving in traffic helps with depth perception between vehicles, especially when performing convoy operations where speeds change constantly and can stop with no warning. This training should be closely monitored by vehicle commanders and performed in a controlled environment.
- Driving on urban terrain. Drivers face numerous obstacles that require superior navigation skills on urban terrain. Moving on unknown rubbled urban terrain congested with conveyances and people requires experience, patience, and quick reflexes.

6-33. Commanders should design driver courses that test Soldier maneuver skills on and off road. Courses should provide areas that test reaction to enemy ambush, direct, and indirect fires. Use of OIF Lessons Learned should serve as the basis of course design. To accommodate this developers should—

- Set up road cone and engineer tape lined driving lanes to test stand-off between other vehicles and perform urban terrain vehicle turns.
- Test convoy driving at every opportunity.
- Test Soldier reactions using simulators and simulations.
- Test crew/squad actions on contact.

NOTE: Stryker DVE sensors give drivers maximum fields of view of direction of travel. Portions of the left front corner and most of the right front corner cannot be observed. To overcome these blind spots vehicle crew members must assist drivers in navigating obstacles and making turns, particularly in complex and restricted terrain.

DRIVER DUTIES AND RESPONSIBILITIES

6-34. Stryker drivers must possess extraordinary driving skills. They must be technically and tactically proficient to maneuver on today's varying operational terrain. We sometimes take our drivers for granted. They do their job so well we have tendencies to forget that they have been driving for hours and need rest.

DRIVER FATIGUE

6-35. When fatigued, driver communications may seem at a loss. Driving mistakes such as erratic speed (up and down) and weaving (left to right) may also be noticed. These are just three trigger points that can indicate a driver is tired.

DVE FATIGUE

6-36. Drivers can become so mentally fatigued from watching the DVE while navigating over unknown terrain during night or environmental conditions (natural and man-made) that they can lose their sense of reality.

Convoy and DVE Fatigue

6-37. Driver fatigue is more prevalent during convoy operations than it is during area presence patrols. Staring hour-after-hour at the back of another vehicle can be hypnotic, making driver reaction and reflex actions slow and lethargic. The problem is compounded when drivers are forced to navigate using the DVE with hatches closed. Rotating drivers regularly can solve these driver fatigue problems, but it is not always possible. The next best option is planning stops to rest drivers at every opportunity.

DUTIES AND RESPONSIBILITIES

6-38. Each licensed operator of a vehicle or piece of equipment is expected to—
- Operate vehicles or equipment in a safe and prudent manner.
- Report unsafe operating conditions of vehicles or equipment.
- Report all accidents to his or her supervisor and to the motor pool that dispatched the equipment.
- Comply with all municipal, state, and military motor vehicle or equipment regulations, as required.
- Ensure cargo (including personnel) is properly loaded, secured, and protected from the elements prior to transport.
- Ensure vehicles and equipment is properly secured when left unattended.
- Wear installed restraint systems.
- Back vehicles and use ground guides according to the provisions of AR 385-55 and FM 21-305.
- Inform supervisors if using medication that may adversely affect vision/coordination or cause drowsiness.
- Perform operated equipment inspections before, during, and after operations.

- Follow all operator maintenance outlined in appropriate equipment technical manuals.
- Care for and clean vehicle equipment, tools, and components.
- Ensure vehicles or equipment is properly serviced.
- Ensure security of the vehicle, cargo, and tools.
- At all times, exercise common sense.

DRIVING WITH THE DVE

6-39. Excellent DVE skills are essential for fast and effective combat maneuver. Regular practice of DVE procedures enable Stryker operators to retain DVE navigation skills necessary during limited visibility conditions. The following Stryker DVE driving tips should be considered when maneuvering.

- Do not make DVE adjustments while moving, if image becomes degraded, or when you feel unsafe with the driving situation.
  (1) Notify chain of command of difficulties. Stop and make adjustments to correct the problem, when possible.
  (2) Select and focus on long distance objects, then select close objects to confirm focus, contrast, and brightness of thermal signatures.
- Drive only in the locked azimuth (AZ) and elevation (EL) (level zero degree) position. This provides the greatest range of motion between zero degrees and maximum AZ and EL positions.
- Maintain a safe distance between vehicles during convoy operations.
  - Distance between vehicles is METT-TC dependant.
  - Too much experience is sometimes worse than too little experience.
  - More experienced drivers may push the envelope during movements.
  - Less experienced drivers may become too cautious.
  - Practice is the only answer to fluid movements in battlefield conditions.
- Do not "OUTDRIVE" the DVE.
  (1) Overlooking upcoming hazards can result from looking too far down course.
  (2) Not enough time for hazard reaction can result from driving too fast.
- **Making turns using the DVE.** Because the DVE looks forward, intersecting pathways will disappear from the driver's FOV prior to the vehicle exiting the intersection.
  (1) **Turning technique.** Slow the vehicle to a comfortable turning speed. As the pathway passes off of display, begin counting five seconds (down to one from five), then begin turn.
  (2) Adjust turn rate as path comes back into view on display.
  (3) Adjust count as necessary considering speed turn rate.

DRIVING CONDITIONS

6-40. Optical systems cannot overcome all natural and man-made battlefield conditions, and the odds of a unit operating within conditions that defeat DVE capabilities are not high (7 percent). Strykers outfitted with the AN/VAS-5 have lowered the possibility of defeating the DVE to around 4 percent. The addition of a "high gain mode" feature further reduces the possibility of thermal washout.

6-41. Skills required for operating the DVE are essential for fast and effective use during combat. Regular practices of these procedures help Stryker operators retain the skills necessary to navigate using the DVE. Refer to the driving steps above for all-weather driving conditions.

DRIVING CROSS-COUNTRY

6-42. Today's DVE is much different than "image intensifying" night vision devices of the past. The DVE's thermal capability provides unparalleled flexibility for driving in either day or night conditions. However, it does not provide the depth perception of the human eye. Therefore, when driving in missions involving cross-country terrain, drivers must pay full attention to potential terrain hazards such as:

- Drop-offs.

- Ditches.
- Ravines.
- Eroded "wash-outs".

6-43. These areas generally look darker than the surrounding terrain and can be anywhere from difficult to impossible to determine the depth of the drop. When encountering a suspected drop-off or ditch, drivers should stop prior to the feature (if tactically feasible) and have a ground-guide direct the vehicle around or through the feature. If a ground-guide is not tactically feasible, unknown areas should be approached slowly with caution while adhering to the prescribed vehicle cant.

NOTE: Strykers are naturally top-heavy and not as sure footed as a flat track vehicle. Adding protective armor makes them even more susceptible to tilt and slide on sloping terrain.

6-44. Although reactive armor provides more protection than a slat-armored cage, slat armor does have a proven record of protecting Stryker vehicles from RPGs. In Iraq, the Stryker's unique operational capabilities and its mission-support role required little change in Infantry tactics. However, the addition of protective armor increased the overall weight and width of the Stryker, affecting its maneuverability on and off road. Other effects are added fuel usage, reduction in speed when crossing obstacles and traveling on roadways, and excessive wear and tear on tires and the suspension system.

6-45. Listed below are 11 considerations for Stryker crews operating with reactive or slat armor.

(1) Weight affects the cant of a vehicle, so move slowly over rolling terrain.
(2) Always be mindful of the added weight, height, and width of the Stryker when selecting routes.
(3) Stay off road shoulders as vehicles are susceptible to rolling over.
(4) Drive up or down the forward slope of hills, never along the side of hills.
(5) Search out hardpan surfaces.
(6) If forced to travel over soft ground, stay at one steady speed to avoid bogging down.
(7) Avoid hills and gullies to lessen strain on the power pack and suspension system.
(8) Set tire pressure in accordance with Stryker technical manuals for on- and off-road operation to lessen wear and tear on tires and the suspension system. Low tire pressure is better when traveling on soft terrain. Normal tire pressure is better when on hard surfaces. The driver must make adjustments to the height management system when moving from hard service roads to off-road surfaces to keep wheels from rubbing the hull.
(9) Go around obstacles when possible.
(10) Operational time and distance must be considered when reactive or slat armor is installed. Set up petroleum, oil, and lubricant (POL) resupply points to account for additional fuel use due to additional weight. Also consider reducing speed to lessen fuel consumption and damage to suspension systems.
(11) Send out reconnaissance teams to check bridge crossings. Some have single lanes, most have two, few have more than two. Strykers with reactive armor or slat will in most cases be too heavy or wide to cross. Use ground Soldiers to provide security to the entrance and exit points of bridges. Have VCs ground-guide Strykers across, especially during hours of limited visibility.

DRIVING ON URBAN TERRAIN

6-46. Drivers must pay special attention to street widths and associated traffic (vehicle or pedestrian) in urban or congested areas, and adjust speed for driving with the DVE. A technique for driving in the urban environment is to develop vision "zones" for reacting to potential hazards. For example, the "Four Second Stopping Zone" can be applied by locating an object to the vehicle front and giving a count of four. Four seconds is the amount of time it takes for the vehicle to reach the object. The four-count times the distance in which the vehicle should be able to stop in case of an emergency situation (unexpected obstacles, civilian cross traffic pulling into the driving lane). The four seconds is based on densely populated areas and can be adjusted for greater traffic speeds in less populated areas. When conducting convoy operations, the stopping zone can be extended to prevent convoy vehicles from bunching up.

6-47.   Another challenge to driving with the DVE in urban operations is peripheral view. Assistance may be required from the VC wearing night vision goggles in poorly lit areas to observe objects to the sides of the vehicle. The VC will also communicate with a trail vehicle, especially if his vehicle is required to drive in reverse. These situations should be practiced prior to performing vehicle maneuvers, especially when the DVE is the only means of navigation.

ALL-AROUND SECURITY

6-48. Hatch locations, the remote weapons station (RWS), and protective armor limits all members of the crew the advantage of a 360-degree, clear field of view—with hatches open and Soldiers up. But all-around security is possible when moving with crews or squads onboard by positioning them in the following manner.

- **From Mid-Deck Forward.** VCs view from mid-deck forward. The location of the RWS interferes with total VC viewing of the left side forward to the left corner of the Stryker.
- **From Left Side to Front-Center.** Crew/squad leaders view from the left side to front-center of the Stryker, covering the area of the VC's field of view that the RWS interferes with.
- **From Mid-Deck Back.** Crew/squad members view from mid-deck back.
- **From the Ground.** Soldiers and other Strykers will provide vehicle security when they are on the ground.

NOTE: Prior to movement the VC should move around the outside of the Stryker to locate and note those portions of the vehicle that cannot be observed when the hatches are open and when they are closed. This should be done from all top hatches (driver, RWS, squad leader position, and troop hatches).

This page intentionally left blank.

Chapter 7
STRYKER DRIVER TRAINER

The commander balances Stryker driver training resources and time using the Common Driver Trainer/Stryker Vehicle (CDT/SV) Simulator. Nothing can replace live driving, but the CDT/SV provides initial and sustainment training for little or no cost. Once the commander and master driver assess their unit's proficiency, simulated training can be integrated to "train to maintain" expert driving standards.

SYSTEM AND PURPOSE

7-1.   The CDT/SV is designed to allow driving skills for all of the Stryker variants including the:

- Infantry carrier vehicle (ICV)
- Mortar carrier vehicle (version B) (MCV-B)
- Reconnaissance vehicle (RV)
- Command vehicle (CV)
- Medical evacuation vehicle (MEV)
- Engineer squad vehicle (ESV)
- Antitank guided missile vehicle (AGTMV)
- Fire support vehicle (FSV)
- Nuclear biological chemical reconnaissance vehicle (NBC-RV)
- Mobile Gun System (MGS)

7-2.   The driver/trainer simulator provides initial and sustainment driver training at training institutions and operational installations. The device consists of a simulated vehicle cab, instructor/operator station, a visual system, a 6-degree of freedom (DOF) motion platform system, AAR station, and a computational system.

7-3.   The trainer is designed to provide:

- An environment to facilitate student acquisition of learning analysis training tasks.
- A set of simulation scenarios to provide exposure and re-enforcement of skills. A scenario is a driving exercise consisting of:
    - Defined pathway though a selected database.
    - Specific environmental defaults.
    - Primary learning task objectives.
    - Scripted events.
    - Audio cues for instructor and student.

7-4.   The purpose of the CDT/SV is to train Stryker driver students on all vehicle variants. The CDT/SV provides students with continuous practice of critical driving skills in various weather and visibility conditions. Simulated terrain includes, desert, woodland, urban, mountainous, and frozen.

7-5.   The system database consists of nine task regions. Each region permits students to drive in terrains varying from steep mountains, to flat rural areas, to urban city settings that interact with traffic. Students are exposed to improvised explosive devices (IEDs) and rocket-propelled grenades (RPGs) within built up areas.

TECHNICAL CHARACTERISTICS

7-6. The CDT/SV consists of a Student Training Station (STS), an Instructor/ Operator Station (IOS), and an After-Action Review (AAR) Station. The STS is comprised of a motion platform, three video display unit(s) (VDU) and a driver compartment (vehicle cab). The IOS has the capacity to operate up to six different STSs at one time. The CDT/SV can be set up in the following configurations:

- One Instructor Operation (I/O) station, one AAR station, and one Student Training Station (STS).
- One Instructor Operation (I/O) station, two AAR stations, and two Student Training Stations (STS).
- One Instructor Operation (I/O) Station, four AAR Stations, and four Student Training Stations (STS).
- One Instructor Operation (I/O) Station, six AAR Stations, and six Student Training Stations (STS).

SYSTEM COMPONENTS

7-7. The STS has four major components: the driver station (Figure 7-1), visual system (Figure 7-2), motion system (Figure 7-3), and computer rack (Figure 7-4). The driver station is accessed through the right side of the cab. The station is equipped with a driver seat, dashboard, steering column, communications equipment, instrument panel, and foot controls located on the cab floor. The cab is equipped with a sound system and closed circuit television cameras (CCTV). The assembled STS is shown in Figure 7-5.

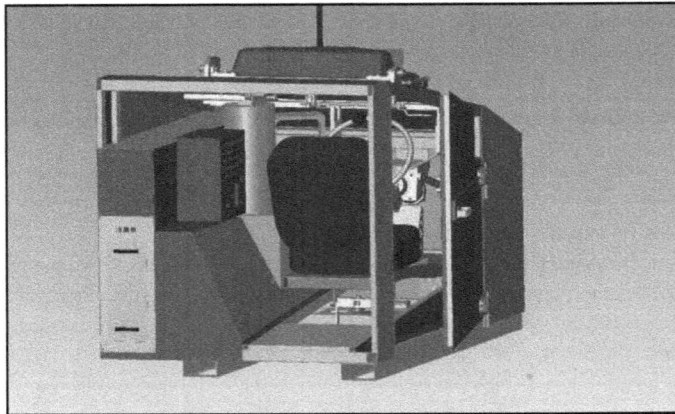

Figure 7-1. Driver station/vehicle cab.

VISUAL SYSTEM

7-8. The simulated training visual environment is created by state-of-the-art computer image generation. Simulator features include synthetic terrain with natural features, buildings, trails, roads, other vehicles, people, and animals. The system can create varying fog, rain, dust, and day or night light levels. Its simulated scenes are displayed on three 60-inch (diagonal measurement) rear-projection monitors. Total forward viewing area is 180°. As the driver maneuvers through a scenario exercise area, autonomous traffic can be utilized. A driver vision enhancer (DVE) is also included in the CDT/SV. The DVE is an LCD screen positioned directly in front of the driver's steering wheel that provides a thermal image in back and white or hot modes of the vehicle front area. The student has an overhead view switch located to the left of the transmission gear selector (Figure 7-2). The overhead view provides a top-down view of the surrounding terrain.

Figure 7-2. Visual system with driver vision enhancer.

MOTION BASE

7-9. The motion base (Figure 7-3) is a device that maneuvers the entire cab assembly. Manual motion base shut down is possible in the event of an emergency. A large red emergency stop button is located in the cab assembly, left of the steering wheel. An additional emergency stop button is located at the IOS. When the button is pressed, the motion base returns to its original start position. The motion base automatically shuts down if the door is opened or if the student is not buckled in. To reactivate the motion system, press pause on the IOS or keypad and press the pause button again to resume.

7-10. The motion base is an important simulation tool that provides driver acceleration and angular cueing. The motion base positions itself as the vehicle travels up and down slopes, giving the driver a sense of being on a slope. It also delivers an initial acceleration feel that slowly returns to zero, and is capable of a limited acceleration feeling that provides the sense of an abrupt forward movement when the vehicle stops. The motion base will deliver the initial acceleration feel and slowly return to zero.

Figure 7-3. Motion base.

STUDENT TRAINING STATION (STS) COMPUTER RACK

7-11. The STS rack (Figure 7-4) contains the STS computer systems, sound generation equipment, image generator(s) (IG), power distribution units, and network switches required to run each Student Training Station (Figure 7-5). Most of the components mounted on the rack are not accessible to the driver or instructor. A qualified maintenance technician should be contacted if the components malfunction. Maintenance personnel are typically located on-site at the user training facility.

Figure 7-4. Student training station computer rack.

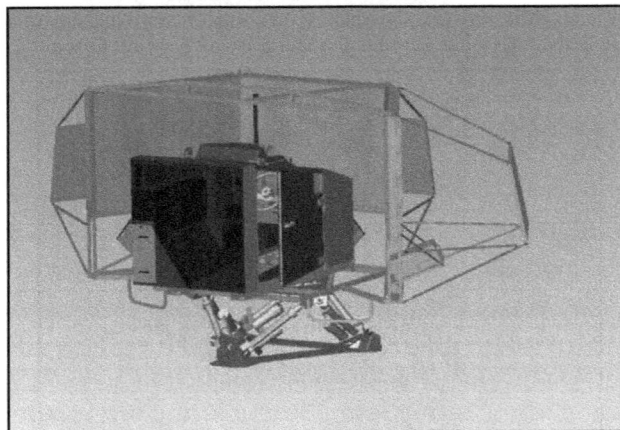

Figure 7-5. Student training station assembly.

7-12. The Instructor/ Operator Station (Figure 7-6) consists of a table, color monitors, closed circuit TV (CCTV) monitors, keyboard, mouse, joystick, and printer.

Figure 7-6. Instructor operator station (IOS).

7-13. A training exercise is set up by selecting the vehicle configuration, traffic conditions, environmental conditions, and scenario. The keyboard is used to enter passwords, instructor and student names, and instructor comments. The mouse is used to navigate through set-up menus, define the conditions, and begin the training exercise. The mouse is also used to monitor and control the simulation, and to stop the exercise.

7-14. The training exercise can be reviewed through a series of score screens that are automatically generated by the simulator. Printed copies of score sheets can also be produced.

7-15. An emergency stop button is located at the IOS. When the emergency stop button is pressed, the motion base will return to its original home position.

INSTRUCTOR OPERATOR STATION (IOS) COMPUTER RACK

7-16. The computer rack (Figure 7-7) located at the IOS contains the IOS computer systems, image generator, power distribution units, and uninterruptible power supply. Most components mounted on the rack are not accessible to the driver or instructor. If the components malfunction, a qualified maintenance technician must be notified immediately. Maintenance personnel are typically located on-site at the user training facility.

Figure 7-7. Instructor operator station (IOS) computer rack.

7-17. The After-Action Review Station is located near the IOS Station. It consists of a table, color monitor, PC, speakers, keyboard, and mouse. The purpose of this station is to allow off-line review of training results after the instructor has halted the training scenario. The AAR GUI supports playback (instant replay) of all or part of the scenario. The instructor is able to pause, rewind, and fast forward (2x, 4x and 8x) the exercise from the AAR GUI page. The playback of a training scenario provides the visual, aural, and instrumentation cues of the original execution through recorded video and sound. AAR capabilities are available only after an exercise has been completed, and are not part of the run-time IOS system. Because it is not part of the run-time IOS system, it can be used in parallel during training sessions.

7-18. Scenarios are arranged according to skill level to provide a core set of scenarios that cover allocated training tasks and supplemental scenarios for re-enforcement and practice. The computer recommends progression based on initial entry parameters and past performance. Soldiers proceed through scenarios and levels at the instructor's discretion.

SKILL LEVEL 1—BASIC BEGINNER DRIVER

7-19. Scenarios at this skill level include:
- Proper start-up and shutdown procedures.
- Basic maneuvering under direction of a ground guide.
- Basic lane and speed control, proper signaling, braking and acceleration, basic right and left turns.

7-20. Scenarios will introduce dual-lane and multi-lane driving situations, parking lot entry, traversing, and exit/entry into traffic.

7-21. Two lane and multi-lane driving situations with traffic control devices are also be presented. So are traffic control devices. Extensive pre-programmed audible voice coaching and instruction is included.

SKILL LEVEL 2—BEGINNER DRIVER

7-22. Scenarios at this skill level include:
- Dual-lane, multi-lane, and controlled access road driving situations.

- Introduction of night and inclement weather conditions (without creating extremely hazardous conditions).
- Backing of the Stryker vehicle in non-tactical situations.
- Driving with indirect driving systems such as DVE vision blocks, and with NBC gear.
- Basics of convoy driving.

7-23. Students are exposed at this level to hazardous condition driving such as vehicle mechanical breakdown, and sudden vehicle or pedestrian entry onto right-of-way. Extensive pre-programmed audible voice coaching and instruction is included.

SKILL LEVEL 3—INTERMEDIATE DRIVER

7-24. Scenarios at this skill level include:

- Basics on urban, interstate highway, and advanced night driving conditions.
- Scenarios that provide a variety of driving experiences replicating all actions learned earlier.
- Backing with a towed load; starting vehicle on upward slope; braking vehicle on downward slope; controlling vehicle with gear selection; and engine brake on downward slope while driving with high CG loads.
- Malfunctions and faults.
- Basics on vehicle handling with all variations of load, armor, and trailer configurations.
- Basics on driving in extreme weather conditions.

7-25. Audible driver commands and coaching for new behaviors are included.

SKILL LEVEL 4—BASIC TACTICAL DRIVER

7-26. Scenarios at this skill level include:

- Cross-country and tactical driving conditions including, sand, desert, mountain, forest, mud, and side slope driving.
- Basics of advanced convoy driving.
- Basics of water fording.
- Introduction of transport loading and unloading procedures (rail, aircraft, HET, ship).

7-27. Extensive audible commands (coaching) for new situations and continuous voice commands are included.

SKILL LEVEL 5—TACTICAL DRIVER

7-28. Scenarios at this skill level include:

- Building on Level 4 complexity through the addition of rain, snow, limited visibility, rocky surfaces, and obstacle avoidance/traversal.
- Driving through marked and unmarked mine fields.
- Driving through urban terrain with RPG/IED threats and impacts.

7-29. Extensive audible coaching for new situations and continuous voice commands are included.

SKILL LEVEL 6—VARIANT SPECIFIC DRIVER

7-30. Scenarios at this skill level include an introduction to specific handling characteristics and tasks for each CDT variant.

7-31. The design of each scenario includes:

- A short title: includes brief scenario characteristics.
  - Example: "Dual-Lane Road - Night".
- A scenario number: prefaced by skill level (1-6).

- Example: Scenario Number "1.3c".
- "1" identifies the Basic Beginner skill level.
- "3" represents the third scenario within the Basic Beginner scenario series.
- "P"/"S" appended to number indicates Primary or Secondary.
- Training tasks.

PART 1 - SCENARIO DESCRIPTION
- Scenario overview.
- Learning objectives.
- Performance measurements—criticality range.

PART 2 - SCENARIO CONDITIONS
- Vehicle configuration at start of scenario.
- Visual environment requirements.
- Aural cues.
- Scripted hazards.
- Malfunctions.
- Other scripted events.

PART 3 - DRIVING ROUTE OVERVIEW
- Generic description of proposed driving route:
  - Specific driving distances on selected road type.
  - Traffic control devices.
  - Turns, intersections, traffic circles.

PART 4 - INSTRUCTOR OPERATIONS
- Description of instructor functions:
  - Trainer initialization.
  - Activate scripted events, hazards, and malfunctions.
  - Additional IOS procedural steps.
  - Training steps that require additional emphasis or instructor observation/action.

PART 5 - INSTRUCTOR TO STUDENT SCENARIO BRIEFING
- Safety requirements.
- Learning objectives.
- Scenario overview.
- Performance measurement.

PART 6 - SCENARIO EXECUTION
- Step-by-step scenario procedures and detailed route definition.
- Scripted event, hazard, and/or malfunction activation by the instructor.

CDT TRAINING SCENARIO	SCENARIO NUMBER S-1

SKILL LEVEL: SAMPLE

TITLE: DUAL-LANE ROAD AND CONTROLLED ACCESS HIGHWAY

ITS TASK REFERENCE
3531.01.01 VEHICLE OPERATION ON-ROAD

PART 1   SCENARIO DESCRIPTION

SCENARIO OVERVIEW
Scenario begins with the CDT/SV parked in parking area. The student will inspect/test vehicle controls and indicators, start the vehicle, and operate the vehicle on dual-lane hard surface roads and on a controlled access highway. The environment will include both suburban and urban areas. Visual displays will include clear daylight conditions, typical suburban and urban scenery, autonomous traffic, pedestrians, and standard traffic control markings and devices. Standard aural cues will be used. There will be no scripted events or hazard/malfunction activation by the instructor. The total driving distance is approximately 8 ¾ miles. Estimated scenario time is 20 minutes.

LEARNING OBJECTIVES
Controls and Indicators Test/Inspection
Dual-Lane and Controlled Access Highway Driving
90 Degree Left and Right Turns
Observance of Traffic Markings and Control Devices
Vehicle Operation with Autonomous Traffic and Pedestrians
Vehicle Operation in an Intersection

SCENARIO CONDITIONS

Vehicle Configuration
- All functional cab controls and indicators <u>OPERATIONAL</u>.
- Parking brake control <u>OUT</u>.
- Transmission range selector in <u>"N"</u>.
- Fuel <u>FULL</u>.
- 2-ton load: no towed load.

Visual Environment
- Clear daytime conditions.
- Parking area at the beginning of driving route.
- Typical suburban environment including rolling hillsides, green grass, sparsely populated green trees, and residential/commercial structures.
- Typical urban environment including commercial/residential structures and sidewalks.
- Standard dual and controlled access highway driving lanes with shoulders.
- Speed limit signs on dual-lane road and controlled access highway.
- Overhead road numbers and exits signs on dual-lane and controlled access roads.
- Autonomous traffic present on both dual-lane roads and controlled access highway.
- Standard traffic light.
- Autonomous pedestrians: Stop sign.
- Three-way intersection with traffic light.
- Traffic circle with yield sign.
- Parking area at end of driving route.

Aural Cues
- Student briefing, driving instructions, and error messages throughout the scenario.
- Standard Instructor cues.

Hazards
- None

Malfunctions
- None

Scripted Events
- None

DRIVING ROUTE DESCRIPTION

- Scenario begins in a parking area.
- Vehicle leaves this area onto a dual-lane road for approximately ½ mile.
- Vehicle executes a left turn at the first traffic light and continues on a dual-lane road for approximately 1 ½ miles.
- Vehicle enters a controlled access highway and proceeds east for approximately 4 miles. The vehicle takes the first exit onto a dual-lane road, proceeds approximately 1½ miles, and stops at the first traffic sign at a three-way intersection.
- Vehicle executes a left turn at the intersection and proceeds ½ mile to a yield sign at a traffic circle.
- Vehicle enters the traffic circle and executes the first right turn onto a dual-lane road.
- Vehicle proceeds approximately ½ mile to a three-way intersection and stops.
- Vehicle executes a left turn onto a dual-lane road and proceeds approximately ¼ mile to the first stop sign.
- Vehicle executes a right turn onto a dual-lane road and parks the vehicle in an available parking slot next to a commercial building on the right side of the road. The scenario is complete at this point.

MAP

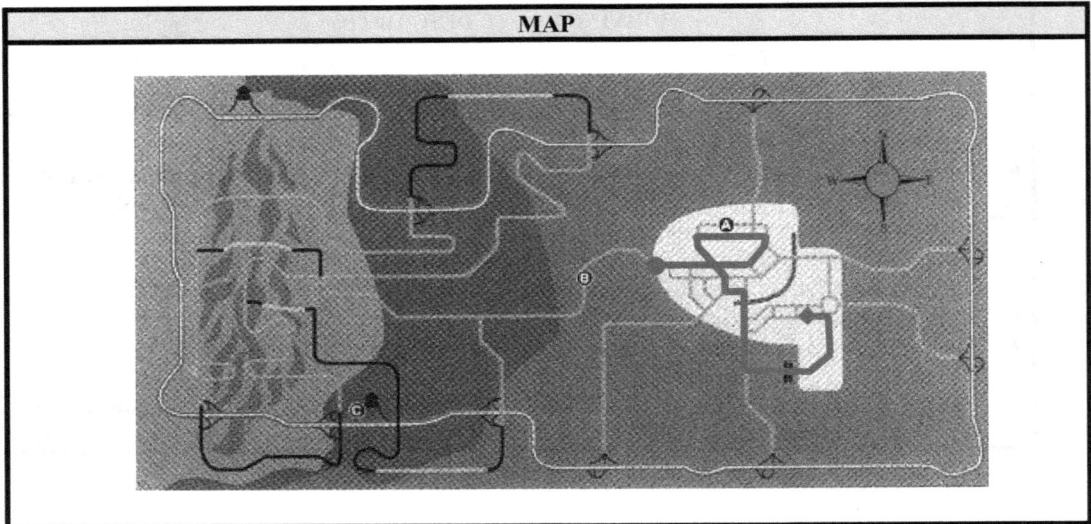

STEP	DRIVING INSTRUCTIONS	DRIVING ROUTE
1	<ul><li>Start the vehicle.</li><li>Exit the parking area to the right.</li><li>Proceed to the first traffic light.</li></ul>	<ul><li>Standard dual-lane road.</li><li>Distance to traffic light approximately ½ mile.</li></ul>
2	<ul><li>Brake and stop the vehicle at the traffic light.</li><li>Execute a left turn.</li><li>Proceed to the first dual-lane road exit.</li></ul>	<ul><li>Standard dual-lane road.</li><li>Distance to exit sign approximately 1 ½ miles.</li></ul>
3	<ul><li>Slow the vehicle and exit the dual-lane road.</li><li>Enter the controlled access highway.</li><li>Proceed to the first dual-lane road exit.</li></ul>	<ul><li>Standard controlled access highway.</li><li>Distance on controlled access highway approximately 4 miles.</li></ul>
4	<ul><li>Slow the vehicle and exit the controlled access highway onto a dual-lane road. Proceed to the first observed traffic sign.</li><li>Brake and stop the vehicle at the traffic sign.</li></ul>	<ul><li>Standard dual-lane road.</li><li>Distance to traffic sign approximately 1 ½ miles.</li></ul>
5	<ul><li>Execute a left turn onto the dual-lane road and proceed.</li><li>Slow and stop the vehicle at the first yield sign.</li><li>Execute a right turn into the traffic circle.</li><li>Execute a right turn from the traffic circle onto the first dual-lane road.</li></ul>	<ul><li>Standard dual-lane roads.</li><li>Distance to traffic circle yield sign approximately ½ mile.</li></ul>

7-32. Basic Beginner Scenario Specifications

- 2.1   Dual-Lane Road Introduction
- 2.2   Dual-Lane Road-Lane Control-No Traffic
- 2.3   Dual-Lane Road-Left/Right Turns-Intersections-No Traffic
- 2.4   Dual-Lane Road-Left/Right Turns-Intersections-Lane Control-No Traffic
- 2.5   Dual-Lane Road-Left/Right Turns-Intersections
- 2.6   Dual-Lane Road-Left/Right Turns-Intersections-Lane Control
- 2.7   Dual-Lane Road-Traffic Circle-Lane Control-No Traffic
- 2.8   Dual-Lane Road-Left/Right Turns-Intersections-Lane Control
- 2.9   Multi-Lane Road Introduction
- 2.10   Multi-Lane Road-Left/Right Turns-Intersections-Lane Control
- 2.11   Multi-Lane Road-Left/Right Turns-Intersections-Lane Control
- 2.12   Multi-Lane Road-Left/Right Turns-Intersections-Lane Control
- 2.13   Multi-Lane Road-Left/Right Turns-Intersections-Lane Control
- 2.14   Multi-Lane Road-Left/Right Turns-Intersections-Lane Control

7-33. Beginner Scenario Specifications

- 2.1   Dual-Lane Road-Traffic Circle-Left/Right Turns-Intersections-Night
- 2.2   Dual-Lane Road-Left/Right Turns-Intersections-Light Fog
- 2.3   Multi-Lane Road-Left/Right Turns-Intersections-Lane Control-Night
- 2.4   Urban Driving Introduction
- 2.5   Urban Driving-Traffic Conditions
- 2.6   Multi-Lane Road -Light Rain
- 2.7   Controlled Access Highway Introduction
- 2.8   Controlled Access Highway-Traffic Conditions
- 2.9   Controlled Access Highway-Convoy Training
- 2.10   Controlled Access Highway-System Malfunction
- 2.11   Controlled Access Highway-Night
- 2.12   Narrow Lane Road Introduction
- 2.13   Narrow Lane Road-Traffic Conditions
- 2.14   Multi-Lane Road-Light Rain and Fog
- 2.15   Reverse Driving-Sight and Blind Side
- 2.16   Reverse Driving-Parking
- 2.17   Reverse Driving-Loading Dock
- 2.18   Reverse Driving-Maintenance Bay
- 2.19   Reverse Driving-Night

7-34. Driver Scores

- Based on currently used road test and skills test.
- Computer and instructor scoring.
  - Computer scores quantitative objectives.
  - Instructor scores qualitative objectives or items that will be impossible to score with the computer.
- Demerit system.
  - Start with 100 points and deduct for each infraction.
- Tunable/tailorable scoring modifiers.

This page intentionally left blank.

Chapter 8

Driving with Slat Armor

Most Stryker variants share similar driving characteristics. These common characteristics change significantly when additional equipment and armor packages are added. This chapter deals with the most performance altering piece of equipment that is regularly added to the Stryker vehicle: the slat armor package.

SLAT ARMOR

8-1.   The add-on system that will most affect the Stryker's driving characteristics is the slat armor package. As shown is the pictures below (Figures 8-1 and 8-2), slat armor consists of a series of steel cage-like panels that surround the vehicle. Each panel is mounted on the body of the Stryker using steel mounting hardware. This increases the length of the Stryker by 1 1/2 feet and the width by 1 1/2 feet. These panels each have different weights, but the entire slat system adds approximately 4,920 pounds to the weight of the vehicle.

Figure 8-1. Slat armor package.

Figure 8-2. Slat armor package.

8-2. The combination of weight and increased size of the vehicle, coupled with how the slat armor package is mounted, significantly changes Stryker vehicle driving characteristics. Affected areas include how it reacts to quick maneuvers, its ability to maneuver through confined areas, and rapid stopping ability. Units should train slat armor driving in confined driving areas with experienced Stryker drivers assisting as a ground guides.

SLAT ARMOR PMCS

NOTE: The slat armor preventative maintenance checks and services (PMCS) is a supplemental to the vehicle PMCS. When slat armor is installed, both vehicle and armor PMCS must be used.

FRONT OF VEHICLE

8-3. Drivers visually check the vehicle front for damage and loose or missing hardware. They also inspect some mounting bolts for looseness. If bolts are loose, they tighten. Maintenance should tighten the mounting bolts to the proper torque value at the first opportunity.

LEFT SIDE OF VEHICLE

8-4. Drivers visually check the left side of the vehicle for damage and loose or missing hardware. They also inspect some mounting bolts for looseness. If bolts are loose, they tighten. Maintenance should tighten the mounting bolts to the proper torque value at the first opportunity.

REAR OF VEHICLE

8-5.   Drivers visually check the rear of the vehicle for damage and loose or missing hardware. They also inspect some mounting bolts for looseness. If bolts are loose, they tighten. Maintenance should tighten the mounting bolts to the proper torque value at the first opportunity.

RIGHT SIDE OF VEHICLE

8-6.   Drivers visually check the right side of the vehicle for damage and loose or missing hardware. They also inspect some mounting bolts for looseness. If bolts are loose, they tighten. Maintenance should tighten the mounting bolts to the proper torque value at the first opportunity.

TIRE PRESSURE (PSI) WITH SLAT ARMOR INSTALLED

8-7.   For highway (primary road) operations/marches, the Central Tire Inflation System (CTIS) must be turned "OFF". Tires must be inflated to 95 psi; vehicle speed must not exceed 45mph. This maximum speed is for ideal road conditions (straight sections with no visible obstructions). Drivers must use common sense and reduce speed when road conditions are not ideal. Weather conditions, an increase in traffic, reduced road width, turns/curves, hillcrests, and adverse terrain are all potentially dangerous conditions. For cross-country movement requiring greater traction (soft soil, mud, or snow) and slow speeds, switch the CTIS "ON" at 61 psi and select "HIGHWAY" setting (81psi) as required by METT-T. When the CTIS is "ON" at 81 psi, a dash up to 40 mph for 1-hour duration is acceptable. For terrain ranging from cross-country to secondary roads, the ICV may be driven with the CTIS "ON" at 81 psi. This CTIS setting should also be required by METT-T and the unit commander's judgment. With resumed extended secondary road movement as soon as the tactical situation permits, the CTIS should be switched "OFF" and the tires inflated to 95 psi.

INSTALLATION

8-8.   Slat armor is installed as a team effort of the vehicle crew and interim contract logistics support (ICLS). The weight of slat armor (4,920Lbs) and height of the vehicle places tremendous strain on crews when installing the armor on more than one vehicle. Environment (hot or cold) can also slow down the process and cause injury due to fatigue from around-the-clock assembly. To assist in the safety and assembly of slat armor, include generators for night assembly and air compressors for impact wrenches.

SET UP WORK DETAILS

8-9.   Handling and installing slat armor will wear down installers. Installers should therefore be rotated regularly to lesson safety hazards to personnel and equipment. A minimum of three personnel are required for installation due to the weight of panels and plates. Store Stryker components that cannot be reinstalled with slat armor installed.

INSTALL SLAT ARMOR IN STAGES TO SAVE TIME

8-10. A simple thumb-nail sketch of armor assembly follows:
    (1) Prepare the vehicle.
    (2) Mount plating.
    (3) Install brackets.
    (4) Install armor.
    (5) Replace components that were taken off.
    (6) Configure load plan.
    (7) Pick up Soldiers and move out.

MANEUVERABILITY

8-11. When equipped with slat armor, Stryker off-road vehicle operation increases tire/ suspension system wear and fuel usage. The increased vehicle size produced by slat armor also affects Stryker maneuverability when traveling on roadways and crossing bridges. Following are driving instructions for slat-armor equipped Stryker off-road operations:

- For highway (primary road) operations/marches, the Central Tire Inflation System (CTIS) must be turned "OFF". Tires must be inflated to 95 psi and vehicle speed must not exceed 45 mph. Maximum speed is for ideal road conditions (straight sections, no visible obstructions).
- For cross-country movement requiring greater traction (soft soil, mud, or snow) and slow speeds, switch the CTIS "ON" and select "HIGHWAY" setting (81 psi) as required by METT-T factors. With the CTIS "ON" at 81 psi, a dash up to 40 mph for a 1-hour duration is acceptable.
- For terrain ranging from cross-country to secondary roads, the ICV may be driven with the CTIS "ON" at 81 psi. Again, this is directed by METT-T and the unit commander's judgment. With resumed extended secondary road movement and as soon as the tactical situation permits, the CTIS should be switched "OFF" and the tires inflated to 95 psi.

OFF-ROAD OPERATION

8-12. When moving off-road, slat-armored Stryker weight effects cant. Drivers should move slow over rolling terrain and remain situation-aware of ground to be covered.

- Reconnoiter through the use of maps and dismounted elements will provide situational understanding on routes to be taken.
- Avoid road shoulders.
- Move up or down the forward slope of hills, never along the side of hills.
- Search out hardpan surfaces.
- If forced to travel over soft ground, one steady speed should maintained to avoid bogging down. Move slower on rough terrain.
- Hills and gullies should be avoided to lessen strain on the Stryker power pack and suspension system.

CROSSING OBSTACLES

8-13. Obstacles should be moved around to save the time it would take to prepare obstacles for crossing. Additional weight can force units to travel only hard surface roads to slowdown additional tire wear and strain on the power pack and suspension system.

- Movement should be slower on rough terrain.
- Hills and gullies should be avoided to lessen strain on the power pack and suspension system.
- Set up petroleum, oil, and lubricant (POL) convoys and re-supply points.

REQUIRE BRIDGE SUPPORT

8-14. Some brides have single lanes. Most have two. Very few have more than two. In most cases, Strykers with slat armor will be either too heavy or wide to cross.

- Infantry will have to dismount and provide security to the entrance and exit points of bridges.
- The vehicle commander may have to walk the vehicle across, especially during hours of limited visibility when driver vision is impaired by slat armor placement.
- Operational time and distance must be considered when slat armor is installed. Reduction in speed will lesson damage to the suspension system and fuel consumption.

SLAT ARMOR-EQUIPPED STRYKER RECOVERY OPERATIONS

8-15. Recovery operations are limited due to close proximity of two Stryker vehicles when slat armor is installed (on the front and rear ramp of towing and towed vehicles). Drivers must be trained on towing procedures to keep from damaging the towing bar, breaking towing pintles, and damaging or dislodging slat armor boxes. Training should include:

- Turning around.
- Performance of an 8-point turn-around.
- Backing up and crossing rolling terrain.

TWO-PIECE TOW BAR

8-16. Towing Strykers with slat armor requires the use of the new two-piece tow bar. The standard tow bar issued for normal Stryker use can cause damage due to turning capability and added space when armor is added.

SLAT ARMOR-EQUIPPED STRYKER VEHICLE OPERATION

HEIGHT MANAGEMENT SYSTEM WITH SLAT ARMOR INSTALLED

8-17. To keep wheels from rubbing the hull, drivers must make adjustments to the height management system when moving from hard service roads to off road surfaces.

OPERATION OF HATCHES AND RAMP WITH SLAT ARMOR INSTALLED

8-18. Hatches should be held when opening and closing to eliminate undue stress on hatch springs, latches, and hinge supports. Care should be taken while opening and closing vehicle hatches when the vehicle is parked on a slope. Gravity and the weight of the hatch can pull personnel out and can crush them against the side of the hull.

OPERATION OF RAMP WITH SLAT ARMOR INSTALLED

8-19. When the slat-armor equipped Stryker vehicle ramp is being lowered it should not be exited until completely open. Personnel should also stand away during the lowering process.

DVE OPERATION

8-20. Finally, drivers and vehicle commanders should be familiar on DVE placement changes when operating the vehicle with or without slat armor.

This page intentionally left blank.

Appendix A
Stryker Vehicle Driver Training Support Packages

Lesson	TLO / ELO
1	**Stryker Driver's Training Introduction and Safety Briefing**
	ELO A: Introduction
	ELO B: Safety Briefing
2	**Identify Characteristics and Major Components of Stryker**
	ELO A: Identify Characteristics and Major Components
3	**Operate Driver's Controls and Instruments on Stryker**
	ELO A: Operate Driver's Controls and Instruments
	Practical Exercise
4	**Operate Driver's Station Before and After Operation**
	ELO A: Prepare Stryker Driver's Station for Operation
	ELO B: Start and Stop the Engine on a Stryker
	ELO C: Operate Auxiliary Power Unit (APU) on a Stryker
	ELO D: Secure Driver's Station on a Stryker
	Practical Exercise
5	**Operate Driver's Vision Enhancer (DVE) on a Stryker**
	ELO A: Identify and Operate the Driver's Vision Enhancer
6	**Operate Ramp on Stryker**
	ELO A: Operate the Ramp on a Stryker
	Practical Exercise

7	Introduction to the Interactive Electronic Technical Manual on Stryker
	ELO A: Introduce the Interactive Electronic Technical Manual (IETM) Capabilities and Features
8	Operate DPMS Functions with the RPDA
	ELO A: Identify the RPDA
	ELO B: Access the ETM-I DPMCS Procedures and Conduct Simulated DPMCS
	Practical Exercise
9	Operate the Intercommunication Set AN/VIC-3 (V) on the Stryker
	ELO A: Operate the Vehicular Intercommunication Set (VIS) AN/VIC-3 (V) on the Stryker
	Practical Exercise
10	Perform Operators Preventative Maintenance Checks and Services (PMCS) on the Stryker Common Chassis
	ELO A: Perform Operator PMCS on the Stryker Common Chassis
	ELO B: Operate Fuel Distribution Assembly on the Stryker
	Practical Exercise
11	Drive Stryker Using Basic Driving Techniques
	ELO A: Use Visual Signaling Techniques
	ELO B: Drive Stryker
	Practical Exercise
	Handouts for Lesson 1
12	Drive Stryker During Day
	ELO A: Drive Stryker
	Practical Exercise

13	**Drive Stryker During Night**
	ELO A: Drive Stryker During Night
	Practical Exercise
14	**Perform Recovery Operations with the Stryker**
	ELO A: Slave-Start a Stryker
	ELO B: Perform Recovery Operations with the Stryker
	ELO C: Tow a Similar Vehicle with the Stryker
	Practical Exercise

This page intentionally left blank.

Appendix B

Sample Stryker Operator/Driver Training Assistance Calendar (10 Day)

B-1. Following is an example Stryker Operator Training Calendar for use in training development. Print it for use in training, or as a guide for developing your own calendar.

DAY & TIME		ACTIVITY	LOCATION	TRAINERS	TEXT REFERENCES	UNIFORM & EQUIPMENT
Day 1						
0900-1000	1.0	**Stryker Drive Orientation Course** Introduction and Safety Briefing	Motor Pool	Unit Trainer	TM 10 Errata, Safety	D
1000-1200	2.0	Identify Characteristics and Describe Major Components / on the **Stryker**	Motor Pool		TM 9-2320-311-10	D
1200-1300	-	Lunch			SOP	D
1300-1600	3.0	Operate Drivers Controls and Instruments on **Stryker**	Motor Pool		TM 9-2320-311-10	D, CVC
1600-1730	1.5	Operate Driver's Station Before and After Operations on **Stryker**	Motor Pool		TM 9-2320-311-10	D, CVC
1730-1800	0.5	Operate Driver's Vision Enhancer (DVE) AN/VAS-5 on **Stryker**	Motor Pool		TM 9-2320-311-10	D, CVC
Day 2						
0900-0930	0.5	Operate Video Display Terminal on **Stryker**	Motor Pool	Unit Trainer	TM 9-2320-311-10	D, CVC
0930-1000	0.5	Operate Ramp on **Stryker**	Motor Pool		TM 9-2320-311-10	D, CVC
1000-1100	1.0	Operate Vehicular Intercommunication Set (VIS) AN/VIC-3(V) on the **Stryker**	Motor Pool		TM 9-2320-311-10	D,CVC
1100-1200	1.0	Perform CrewDrills on **Stryker**	Motor Pool		TM 9-2320-311-10	D
1200-1300	-	Lunch			SOP	D
1300-1330	.0.5	Perform CrewDrills on **Stryker**	Motor Pool		TM 9-2320-311-10	D, CVC
1330-1600	2.5	Perform Operators Preventive Maintenance Checks and Service/RPDA (PMCS) on **Stryker**	Motor Pool		TM 9-2320-311-10	D, CVC
1600-1800	2.0	Operate Driver's Station Before and After Operations EVALUATION on **Stryker**	Motor Pool		TM 9-2320-311-10	D, CVC
Day 3						
0700-1200	5.0	Driver **Stryker** Using Basic Driving Techniques Day (Stop, Start, Steer #1)	Motor Pool	Unit Trainer	TM 9-2320-311-10	D, CVC
1200-1300	-	Lunch			SOP	D
1300-1800	5.0	Drive **Stryker** During Day (Drive on Secondary Roads) (8.0 Day/2.0 DVE)	Motor Pool		TM 9-2320-311-10	D, CVC
Day 4						
0700-1200	5.0	Driver **Stryker** During Day (Drive on Secondary Roads)	Motor Pool	Unit Trainer	TM 9-2320-311-10	D, CVC
1200-1300	-	Lunch			SOP	D
1300-1700	4.0	Drive **Stryker** During Day (Drive on Secondary Roads)	Motor Pool		TM 9-2320-311-10	D, CVC
1700-1800	-	Dinner			SOP	D
1800-2400	6.0	Drive **Stryker** During Night (Drive Secondary Roads) (9.0 Day/6.0 Night DVE)	Motor Pool		TM 9-2320-311-10	D, CVC
Day 5						
0900-1200	3.0	Drive **Stryker** During Day (Drive on Secondary Roads)/ Perform Recover Operations with the **Stryker**	Motor Pool	Unit Trainer	TM 9-2320-311-10	D, CVC
1200-1300	-	Lunch			SOP	D
1300-1800	5.0	Drive **Stryker** During Day (Drive on Secondary Roads) (6.0 Day/2.0 DVE)	Motor Pool		SOP TM 9-2320-311-10	D, CVC

Sample Stryker/Operator Driver Training Assistance Calendar (10 Day)

DAY & TIME		ACTIVITY	LOCATION	TRAINERS	TEXT REFERENCE	UNIFORM & EQUIPMENT
Day 6						
0700-0730	0.5	Perform Operators Preventive Maintenance Checks and Services on Stryker (PMCS) on the Stryker	Motor Pool	Unit Trainer	TM 9-2320-311-10	D
0730-1200	4.5	Drive Stryker During Day (Drive on Secondary Roads)	Training Area		TM 9-2320-311-10	D, CVC
1200-1300	-	Lunch			SOP	
1300-1700	4.0	Drive Stryker During Day (Drive on Secondary Roads)	Training Area		TM 9-2320-311-10	D, CVC
1700-1800	-	Dinner			SOP	
1800-2400	6.0	Drive Stryker During Night (Drive on Secondary Roads)	Training Area		TM 9-2320-311-10	D,CVC
		(5.5 DAY – 9.0 Night/DVE)				
Day 7						
0900-0930	0.5	Perform Operators Preventive Maintenance Checks and Services (PMCS) on the Stryker		Unit Trained		
0930-1200	2.5	Drive Stryker During Day				
1200-1300	-	Lunch				
1300-1800	5.0	Drive Stryker During Day	Training Area		TM 9-2320-311-10	D,CVC
		(5.5 DAY – 2.0 DVE)				
Day 8						
0700-0730	0.5	Perform Operators Preventive Maintenance Checks and Services on Stryker (PMCS) on the Stryker	Motor Pool	Unit Trainer	TM 9-2320-311-10	D
0730-1200	4.5	Drive Stryker During Day (Drive on Secondary Roads)	Training Area		TM 9-2320-311-10	D, CVC
1200-1300	-	Lunch			SOP	
1300-1700	4.0	Drive Stryker During Day (Drive on Secondary Roads)	Training Area		TM 9-2320-311-10	D, CVC
1700-1800	-	Dinner			SOP	
1800-2400	6.0	Drive Stryker During Night (Drive on Secondary Roads)	Training Area		TM 9-2320-311-10	D,CVC
		(5.5 DAY – 9.0 Night/DVE)				
Day 9						
0700-0730	0.5	Perform Operators Preventive Maintenance Checks and Services (PMCS) on the Stryker	Motor Pool	Unit Trainer	TM 9-2320-311-10	D, CVC
0730-1200	4.5	Drive Stryker During Day (Obstacles / Drive Cross Country)	Training Area		TM 9-2320-311-10	D, CVC
1200-1300	-	Lunch (Stop, Start, Steer #2)			SOP	D
1300-1700	4.0	Drive Stryker During Day (Obstacles / Drive Cross Country)	Training Area		TM 9-2320-311-10	D, CVC
1700-1800	-	Dinner (Stop, Start, Steer #2)			SOP	
1800-2200	4.0	Drive Stryker During Night	Training Area		TM 9-2320-311-10	D CVC
		5.5 DAY – 7.0 NIGHT/DVE				
Day 10						
0900-0930	0.5	Perform Operators Preventive Maintenance Checks and Services (PMCS) on the Stryker	Motor Pool Training Area		TM 9-2320-311-10	D
0930-1200	2.5	Drive Stryker During Day			TM 9-2320-311-10 SOP	D, CVC
1200-1300	-	Lunch			SOP	D
1300-1800	5.0	Drive Stryker During Day	Training Area		TM 9-2320-311-10	D,CVC
		(4.5 DAY – 3.0 DVE)				

Notes:

- All driving can be conducted with or without SLAT Armor
- Times are approximations and will be influenced by the student-instructor ratio (four-one used for planning purposes) and the capability of the students to acquire the skills being trained.
- Driving Times per Soldier:

    12.3 Hours Day and 10 Hours Night/D VE

    TOTAL 22.3Hours

- **PMCS** will be performed every day before Driving.
- It is recommended that unit Master Drivers/licensed Stryker Drivers conduct Training during Days 5-10

Uniform

	Description
D	Duty
CVC	Combat Vehicle Crewman Helmet
M40/M42	Protective Masks

Unit Requirements:

1. Kevlar
2. NBC Mask
3. DA 348

Resources Requirements:

1. Training Area
2. Driver's Course

APPENDIX C

STRYKER DRIVER TRAINING COURSES

This appendix provides design standard recommendations for three expert-level Stryker driver training courses.

OVERVIEW

C-1. A critical element of Stryker training is to teach safe driving. Because the Stryker is a significantly different platform than many Soldiers have ever operated, it is crucial that they feel confident negotiating many skilled driving tasks on varying types of terrain. Tasks should include, climbing and descending steep inclines, negotiating obstacles, and maneuvering through confined, curvy areas.

STRYKER DRIVER TRAINING COURSES

STANDARDS AND LAYOUTS

C-2. Soldier driving proficiency is directly related to the ability of an installation to provide diverse driving conditions during training. To accommodate this, standard course design guidelines are outlined below. Every effort should be made to develop driver training courses using these standards. Installations that cannot accommodate all appendix standards may improvise course development. Natural obstacles can be used where they suffice. Employment evaluations of improvised obstacles must be based on their physical abilities to endure repeated use.

STOP, START, AND STEER COURSE

C-3. The stop, start, and steer course (Figure C-1) provides for the training of fundamental driving skills. The course layout is designed to train and enhance the skills of starting, stopping, and steering the Stryker vehicle. The course is approximately 500 meters by 500 meters with a driving lane that is about 16 feet wide. The course has designated areas for each of the tasks being trained. An example of this course layout and design is shown in figure C-1.

DRIVING COURSE

C-4. The driving course (Figure C-2) is the next logical progression for driver training. This course enables drivers to maneuver the Stryker over a distance. The driving course should be no less than 15 miles in length with three alternate routes encompassed within the master loop.

URBAN/OBSTACLE DRIVING COURSE

C-5. The urban and obstacle course (Figure C-3) provides training for advance driving skills. As the world becomes more urbanized it will become necessary for Sryker drivers to posses the skills necessary to maneuver the vehicle in close quarters and through a variety or obstacles. The urban and obstacle course should contain a variety of areas designed to challenge the skills of even the most experienced drivers. Commanders may modify or alter the recommendation design of an urban/obstacle driving course based on uniqueness's of their area of operation. Course design recommendations follow.

- Minimum of one (1) step-up/wall (Figure C-4). Four feet across, 3 feet deep, 10 feet wide with Concrete, steel reinforced edges.
- Minimum of one 18-inch high, 10-foot wide trench. Must include a concrete pad not less than 15 feet in front of and after the step-up. Trench should have steel reinforced edges (Figure C-5).
- Minimum of one 40 percent slope climb and descend.
- Depth of obstacle no less than 25 meters in length.
- Not more than 60 percent slope.

- A series of six bumps or moguls in depth. Each bump/mogul should be:
    - Not less than 24-inches high, but not greater than 36 inches.
    - Not less than 48-inches thick.
    - Width of each bump or mogul not less than 108 inches in length.
    - Not less than 48 inches between each bump/mogul.
- Not less than 500 meters of confined space driving. Area should include:
    - Wooded area.
    - Urban area.
    - Man-made area (connexes).
    - No more than 18 inches clearance on either side of the vehicle (including when fitted with add-on or slat armor).
- Driving area with not less than a 10 percent side slope.
    - Depth of obstacle not less than 10 meters in length.
    - Not more than 30 percent side slope.
    - Must have gradual entrance and exit to obstacle.
- Not less than 300 meters of consecutive tight turns (hair-pin) in a confined area.
    - Fifty (50) percent must be left hand turns.
    - Fifty (50) percent must be right hand turns.
- Two (2) percent of the loop distance to be hard surface road driving.
- Twenty-five (25) percent of this loop to be high speed (40 mph) driving.
- Three (3) percent of the loop distance to be unimproved road driving.
- Balance of the loop to be cross-country driving.
- Fifty (50) percent of driving time to be conducted under limited visibility conditions w/ DVE.

C-6. The execution of all drivers course should follow the guidelines outlined below:
- Course will be negotiated by primary vehicle driver and alternate vehicle driver and
- Vehicle commanders will operate the Stryker at a minimum of one time during daylight hours.
- Drivers will be buttoned up.
- Dismounted: Vehicle Commander will be on the ground, guiding his driver through the course.
- Mounted: Vehicle Commander will be on the vehicle guiding his driver through the course, talking to the driver through the CVC.
- Course will be negotiated both day and during hours of limited visibility.
- Drivers will continue to go through the course until the instructor is satisfied with the driver's proficiency.
- For optimal results, course should be set up on both hilly and flat terrain.
- Six (6)-to-8 foot pylons should used to canalize the course (Figure C-6).

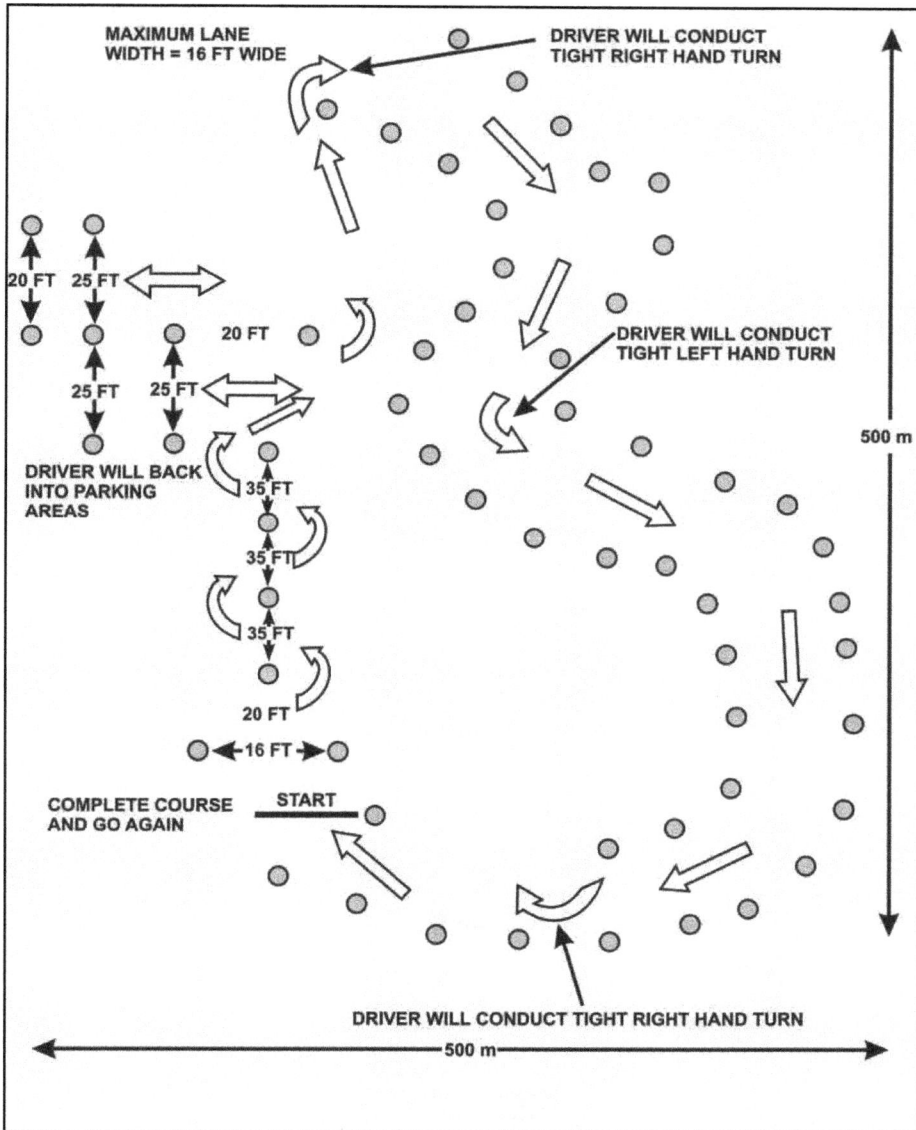

Figure C-1. Stop, start, steer course layout.

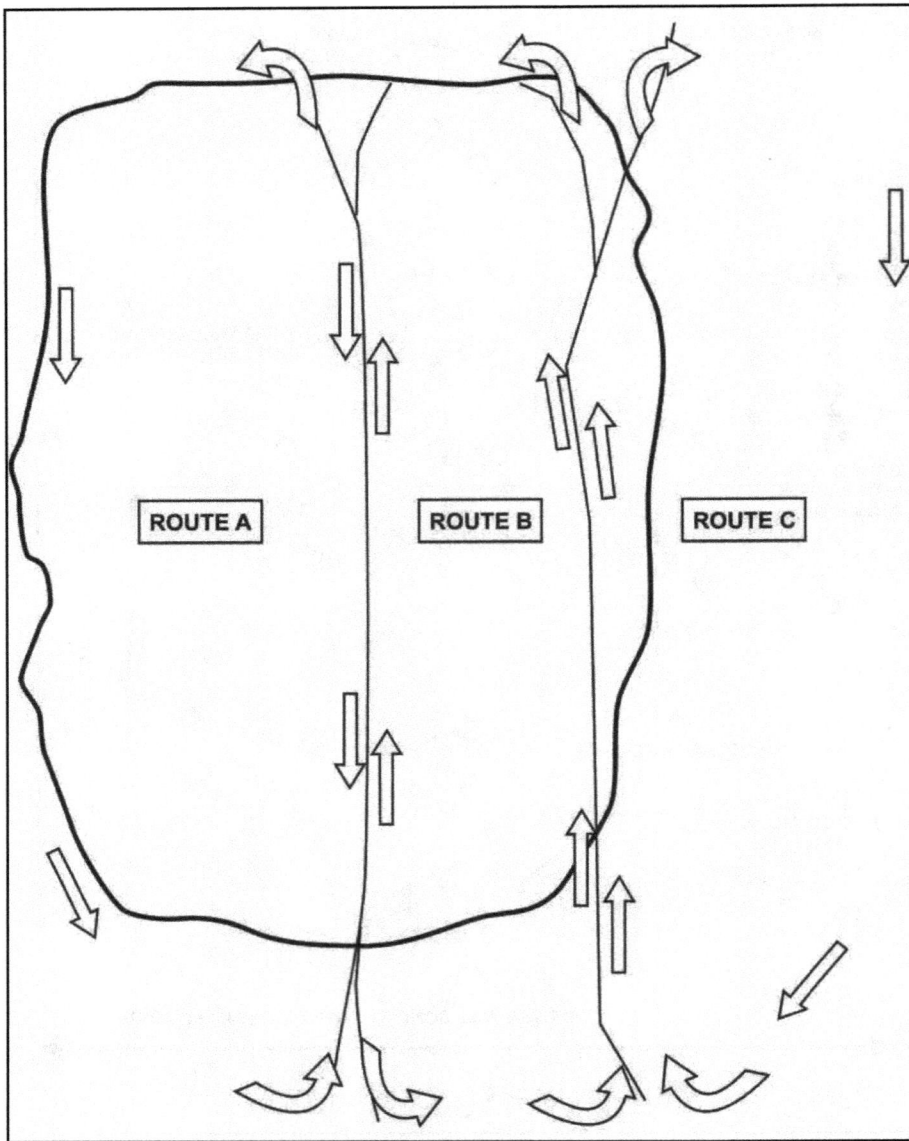

Figure C-2. Driving course.

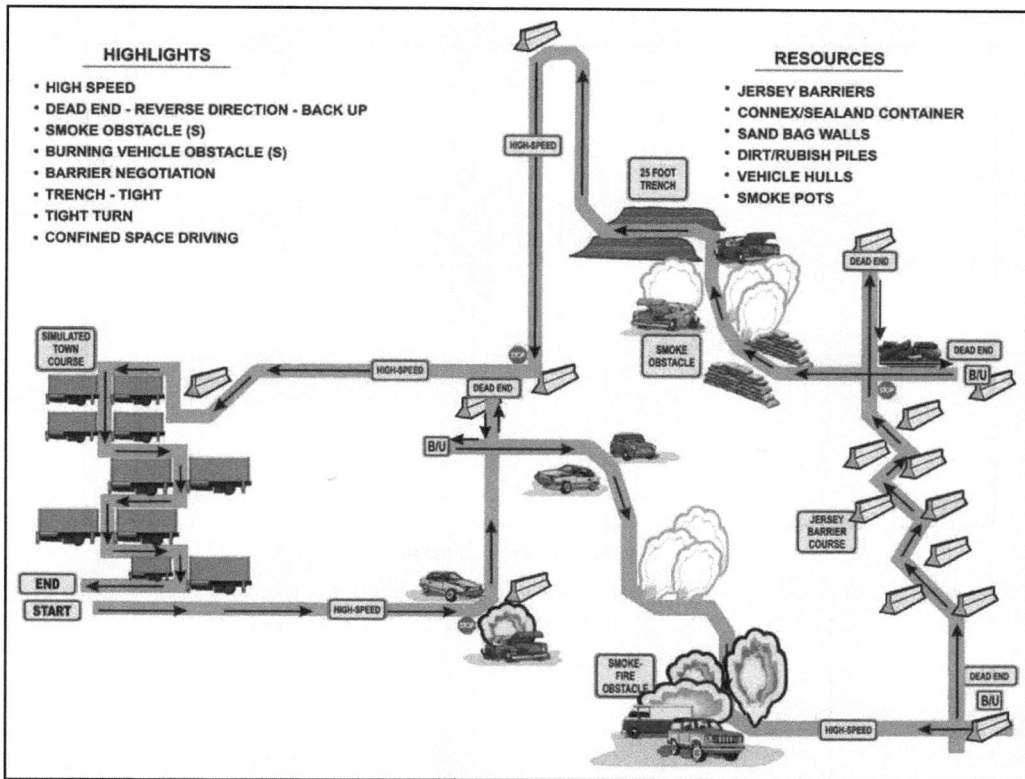

Figure C-3. Urban obstacle drivers course (example).

C-7.   Orange traffic cones with 6-to-8 foot wooden doweling sticking out of the top of the cone provide a good, inexpensive option for conducting this type of driving course. The ground guide should initially guide the driver through the obstacles using standard hand and arm signals. This will give the new driver an idea of how wide the vehicle is, and what he must do to compensate for the difference in driving characteristics. The driver should then be directed to move through the obstacles slowly by themselves, providing feedback as they maneuver through the course.

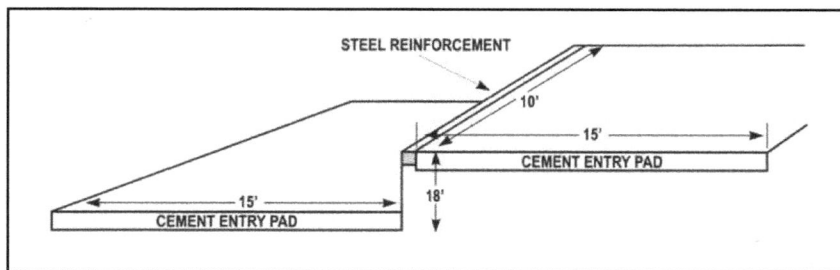

Figure C-4. Step-up/wall (example).

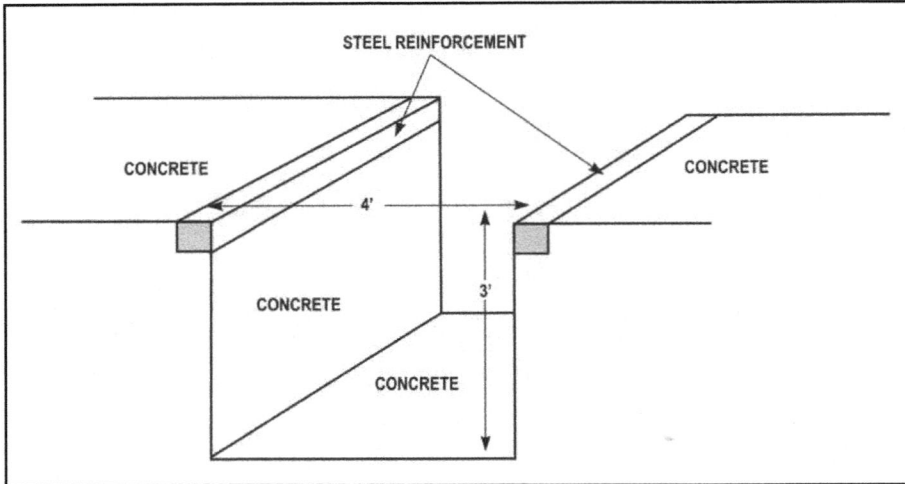

Figure C-5. Trench (example).

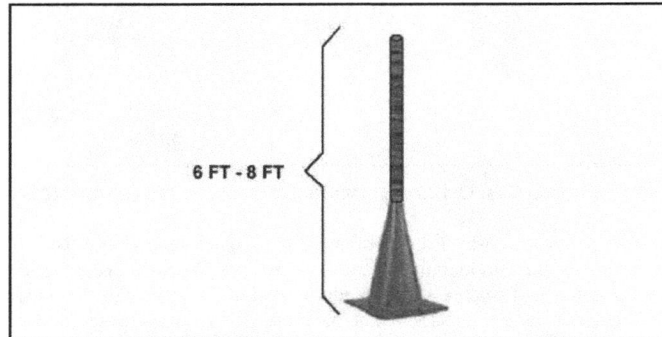

Figure C-6. 6-to-8 foot course pylons.

Appendix D
LESSONS LEARNED

The lessons learned in this appendix come from a U.S. Marine Corps light armored vehicle (LAV) unit serving in Operation Iraqi Freedom. Stryker operators and leaders can benefit because of LAV and Stryker similarity, and LAV lessons learned in urban environments.

ATTACK AND MOVEMENT

D-1. Despite current SOP, vehicle commanders (VCs) fought out of the hatch "popped up" 99 percent of the time. They did this for three reasons: all-around visibility; safety; and target acquisition. The LAV used by the USMC is a high center of gravity vehicle.

D-2. Though the vehicle can maneuver straight up a 60 percent slope, it can only traverse a 30 percent slope. Fighting holes, dips, and steep road shoulder drops proved to be major problems. While drivers drove buttoned up 90 percent of the time, and always during movement to contact, the field of view was so narrow that VCs were required to give detailed commands with regard to obstacles and hazards. As for target acquisition, there are no independent thermal or optical sights for the VCs. Therefore, VCs were limited to what the gunner saw, or what they saw through periscopes arrayed around the hatch. Periscopes reduce visibility and reaction times to a threat by 50-60 percent. Therefore, unless indirect fire was impacting directly on the LAV's position, they did not button up.

D-3. In Tikrit, the Lessons Learned commander's platoons (four vehicles apiece with approximately three to four scouts each) were faced with clearing several city blocks that often left individual vehicles isolated. They were not digitized at the vehicle level. The vehicles crept forward as the scouts moved, never letting the scouts get out of sight for the sake of protecting both the scouts and the vehicles. The scouts cleared every corner and intersection before their vehicle crossed. While the gunner scanned between the first and second floors of buildings, the VCs covered the rooftops. Before scouts dismounted the vehicles, all scout hatches were closed to keep grenades out.

D-4. Observation alternated between the vehicle's thermal sight and night vision goggles because action in Afghanistan proved that continuous use of the "thermals" burned up sensor units quickly. We were fortunate when we attacked into Tikrit, because the resistance was very light. "The times have changed now, and if we did it over again against the threat in place now, we'd be more deliberate in movement."

MOVING WITHIN URBAN AREAS

D-5. The Division zone stretched from An Nasireyah in the south, to Al Hillah in the north. This comprised a distance of approximately 300 miles with only one improved highway (MSR Tampa – Route 1) running through the middle of it. Many other roads were two lane and unimproved dirt roads where the LAV's speed (and to some degree mobility) advantage was drastically hampered.

D-6. When trying to win "hearts and minds" on Iraq's crowded and narrow urban streets, driving an LAV through the middle of downtown was ineffective at best, and could lead to a "flashpoint" at worst. While the company did experience some minor traffic accidents with Iraqi civilians (they are notoriously aggressive and dangerous drivers), there were no casualties. There were several children killed by high speed U.S. military vehicles during the same time frame…a situation that could have boiled out of control if Marine forces did not have the relationship it did with the local population. The commander made it a point to ensure Bravo Company took great pains to avoid congested civilian traffic areas, especially if the mission or commander's intent allowed for this flexibility. While remaining as unpredictable as possible, the company also avoided morning and afternoon "rush hour" in built up urban environments.

TRAFFIC CONTROL POINTS: STATIONARY, ROVING, AND HASTY

D-7. The company was often assigned the task of rapidly moving to and controlling access through, along, or near major avenues of approach, egress, or heavily traveled main supply routes. This was largely an effort to deter or deny former regime loyalist (FRL) forces the use of these routes or to monitor traffic activity along them. The great benefit of light armored reconnaissance (LAR) was the manner in which it could quickly own a space with point or route security. Its limitation was not having enough dismounted Marines to effectively man traffic control points over a long period of time. This problem was solved by task organizing elements from Lima Company 3/5 with Bravo Company. This combined team gave Battalion Task Force 3/5 a good deal of flexibility when handling a myriad of security challenges along the many improved, unimproved, and dirt roads that crisscrossed its zone. The battalion established numerous stationary and defined checkpoints throughout its zone that Bravo Company and other battalion elements manned on a regular basis.

D-8. Bravo Company also conducted a process of roving and hasty checkpoints. The hasty checkpoints were particularly effective when a suspected vehicle was spotted and a section or platoon of LAVs lying in wait descended upon and searched the vehicle and its occupants. Another effective variation of this technique is called the "squeeze-play". One LAV would set itself overtly at a tactical control point (in a hull down position preferably) on an avenue of approach—with another LAV lying covertly in defilade approximately 200-300 meters from its wingman vehicle. As an Iraqi vehicle approached, a dismounted scout team would position themselves to pull the vehicle over for a search. Most vehicles would comply with the search. However, if they didn't, the nearby LAV could pull forward, and if the Iraqi's vehicle made an abrupt u-turn in an attempted get away, the "squeeze play" vehicle was given a quick radio brevity code to cut off the vehicle attempting to egress. This was especially effective when Bravo Company conducted its force protection mission with BTF 3/5 while conducting stipend payments for former Iraqi Soldiers. Several suspected FRL members were caught along with numerous weapons, ammunition, and bundles of Iraqi and U.S. currency.

THREAT

D-9. An LAV presents a high value and tempting target if a creative dismounted enemy (often using getaway civilian vehicles) can canalize and ambush with a combination of small arms, IEDs, RPGs, and other massed surprised fires in a built up area. Several IEDs were employed against Bravo Company in similar fashion, fortunately without any significant personnel or vehicle damage. In these situations the alertness of the Marines and dispersion of our vehicles was the key to preventing the enemy's success. Following are some driving tips Bravo Company found effective:

- Vary the distance between vehicles and do not create patterns. This helps defeat the enemy's timing when detonating IEDs or leading with RPGs and small arms.
- Employ liberal use of scouts to conduct security sweeps along the flanks of heavily traveled routes prior to moving any vehicles on them. This sounds like a simple concept, but was an incredibly unfamiliar concept with certain units.

D-10. While the congestion, tight spaces, and 360 degree nature of a built-up area may negate the full effectiveness of an LAVs optical and firepower advantages, scouts or attached Infantry should be employed. This will provide maximum standoff and security, and is especially important in a civil disturbance or riot control situation. Creating a buffer between an LAV and an unruly, potentially dangerous crowd is critical. There are not many attractive options for an LAV if it is about to be overrun, even if by a mob of "innocent" civilians. Getting too close to a crowd also affords the enemy the opportunity to engage an LAV from within or nearby those civilians, hoping to draw fire back. LAV intimidation through its imposing presence, faking a charge (lifting the trim-vane has definite shock value), ramming vehicles, or firing warning shots are the only measures an LAV crew can take before employing deadly force.

D-11. Civil unrest operations in An Nasiriyah and Al Hillah provided several lessons learned:

- Create maximum standoff and "buffers" with organic scouts or integrated Infantry to preserve and exploit the LAVs imposing presence.

- Achieve effective coordination between dismounted scouts/Infantry to work as a combined team that maximizes the capabilities of both.
- Have a thorough understanding of the urban ground your unit is working on. A simple map reconnaissance will not do justice to the myriad of streets and alleys present in neighborhoods that are old, dense, and complicated.
- Finally, we must have the ability to quickly maneuver or egress along multiple avenues as the situation and time of day dictate. This is every leader's responsibility. Remember Mogadishu!

This page intentionally left blank.

References

This list of publications includes all material necessary to manage and supervise a Stryker Driver Training program. Reference them for use with TC-21 when developing your unit's Stryker driver training program. Changes to these publications and current publication dates can be found in DA Pam 25-30.

DEPARTMENT OF THE ARMY REGULATIONS

AR 190-5	Motor Vehicle Traffic Supervision. 22 May 2006.
AR 385-10	The Army Safety Program. 29 February 2000.
AR 385-40	Accident Reporting and Records. 01 November 1994.
AR 385-55	Prevention of Motor Vehicle Accidents. 12 March 1987.
AR 600-8-22	Military Awards. 25 February 1995.
AR 600-55	The Army Driver and Operator Standardization Program (Selection, Training, Testing, and Licensing). 31 December 1993.
AR 611-5	Army Personnel Selection and Classification Testing. 10 June 2002.

DEPARTMENT OF THE ARMY FORMS

DA Form 348	*Equipment Operator's Qualification Record (Except Aircraft).*
DA Form 2028	*Recommended Changes to Publications and Blank Forms.*

OPTIONAL FORMS

OF 346	*U.S. Government Motor Vehicle Operator's Identification Card.*

FIELD MANUALS

FM 5-0	Army Planning and Orders Production. 20 January 2005.
FM 9-43-2	Recovery and Battle Damage Assessment and Repair. 3 October 1995.
FM 55-30	Army Motor Vehicle Transport Units and Operations. 15 September 1999.
FM 100-14	Risk Management. 23 April 1998 w/change 1, 8 August 2005.

TRAINING CIRCULARS

TC 21-305	Training Program for Wheeled Vehicle Accident Avoidance. 19 August 1996.
TC 21-305-2	Training Program for Night Vision Goggle Driving Operations. 04 September 1998.

GRAPHIC TRAINING AIDS

GTA # 43-01-129	Stryker Cold Weather Operation. 01 June 2006. (Reimer Training and Doctrine Digital Library.)

TECHNICAL MANUAL

TM 9-2355-311-10-1-1, Common Items for Stryker Family of Vehicles. Final Draft. MAR 06. (Published by Tank Armaments Command [TACOM]: Available at Stryker units and through U.S. Army Tank-automotive and Armaments Command, ATTN: AMSTA-LC-CILT, 6501 East Echo 11 Mile Road, Warren, MI 48397-5000).

This publication is available at:
Army Knowledge Online (www.us.army.mil) and
General Dennis J. Reimer Training and Doctrine
Digital Library at (http://www.train.army.mil).

This page intentionally left blank.

Glossary

Acronym/Term	Definition
AAR	after-action review
APU	auxiliary power unit
AR	Army regulation
ATGMV	antitank guided missile vehicle
ATSC	Army Training Support Center
AZ	azimuth
BOT	burst on target
CDT/SV	common driver trainer/Stryker vehicle simulator
CCTV	closed circuit television
CTIS	Central Tire Inflation System
CV	commander's vehicle
CVC	combat vehicle crewman
DA	Department of the Army
DVE	driver vision enhancer
ESV	engineer squad vehicle
FRL	former regime loyalist (forces)
FSV	fire support vehicle
FM	field manual
FOV	field of view
ICLS	interim contract logistics support
ICV	Infantry carrier vehicle
IED	improvised explosive device
IETM	interactive electronic technical manual
IG	image generator, Inspector General
IOS	instructor/operator station
IR	infared
LBE	load bearing equipment
MCV-B	mortar carrier vehicle (version B)
METL	mission essential task list
METT–TC	mission, enemy, terrain and weather, troops and support available, time available, civil considerations
MOS	military occupational specialty
NBC-RV	nuclear, biological, chemical-reconnaissance vehicle
NCO	noncommissioned officer
NET	New equipment training
NVG	night vision goggles
NVD	night vision device
OF	official form

PMCS	preventative maintenance checks and services
POL	petroleum, oil, lubricants
RAWLS	rotating amber warning lights
RPG	rocket-propelled grenade
RWS	remote weapons station
SOP	standing operating procedure
STS	student training station
TAG	test administration guide
TC	training circular
TM	technical manual
TRADOC	United States Army Training and Doctrine Command
TSP	training support package
VDU	video display unit
VIS	vehicular intercommunication set

Index

By Order of the Secretary of the Army:

PETER J. SCHOOMAKER
General, United States Army
Chief of Staff

Official:

JOYCE E. MORROW
Administrative Assistant to the
Secretary of the Army

0633502

DISTRIBUTION:

Active Army, Army National Guard, and U. S. Army Reserve: To be distributed in
electronic media only.

* 9 7 8 1 7 8 0 3 9 9 5 4 6 *